RELIGION OF THE FATHERS

CONTEXT FOR THE BOOK OF ABRAHAM

Denver C. Snuffer, Jr.

Paperback ISBN 978-1-951168-76-6
Hardcover ISBN 978-1-951168-77-3

Copyright © 2021 by Denver C. Snuffer, Jr.
All Rights Reserved

Cover art by David Christenson

Published in the United States by
Restoration Archive LLC

The Restoration Archive website address:
www.restorationarchives.com

Table of Contents

Table of Contents 3
Introduction 5
Preface 7
Prologue 13
Context for the Book of Abraham 15
    Part 1 15
    Part 2 83
THE BOOK OF ABRAHAM 119
    Facsimile 1 119
    Chapter 1 121
    Chapter 2 122
    Chapter 3 124
    Chapter 4 125
    Chapter 5 126
    Chapter 6 128
    Chapter 7 128
    Facsimile 2 134
    Facsimile 3 136
Additional Resources 137

Introduction

The first and most complete religion belonged to Adam and Eve. They lived with God, and after being cast out, they retained a memory of living in God's presence. Adam taught the first eight patriarchs born after him the Religion of the Fathers, which involved direct communion, contact, and connection between mankind and God. It enabled the faithful to hear directly from the Lord His promise of eternal life, to seal them by covenant into His Heavenly Family.

Despite nearly universal apostasy and rebellion against God while Adam lived, the line of first or Patriarchal Fathers preserved the true religion. Their religion was Adam's religion, and their understanding reached back to the Garden of Eden. They experienced visions, ascended into Heaven, obtained promises of exaltation, and were transformed by their experiences from men into angels of God.

After Shem (Melchizedek), an apostasy lasted until Abraham. Although he was raised by an idolater, Abraham searched for the true God of Heaven. He "sought for the blessings of the Fathers," the very thing Malachi prophesies will return before the great and dreadful return of the Lord. Like Adam (at the beginning) and his descendant, Enoch, Abraham was caught up into Heaven and received a tutorial endowment from God. The covenant of the first Fathers was renewed and conferred upon him by Melchizedek, thereby restoring continuity back to Adam.

Abraham represents the key Patriarchal Father prophesied of in Malachi. Abraham not only renewed the covenant of the Fathers (including Noah and Enoch), but also, through the Abrahamic covenant, God established Abraham as the new head of the family of God on Earth.

The Book of Abraham has become a battleground because it is so important for our salvation. Recovering the Religion of the Fathers, becoming of one heart with the Fathers, and fulfilling the prophecy of Malachi are directly connected to Abraham. The more we can learn of Abraham, the more we can know of the covenant with the Fathers spoken of by Malachi, and those same blessings of the Fathers that will be administered again before the end. Therefore, any book written by Abraham should be priceless to us.

This book is more than just a strong defense of the Book of Abraham. What follows also adds significant context and depth to the revelations contained in the Book of Abraham, particularly as they relate to the "strange act" the Lord has undertaken in our day.

After the fall of mankind, for 15 generations from Adam to Shem (Melchizedek), and Abraham to Joseph, the first Fathers were taught they could walk and talk with God, receive answers from Him, and return to His presence. The process of the ascent of man into Heaven to commune with God was always the heart of the true religion. In the end, that process will reverse, and contact between mankind and God will involve the descent of God from Heaven to visit His tabernacle.

The Lord's "strange act" is approaching completion. The promises made to the Fathers are being vindicated. The Restoration has recommenced, and if we are faithful, it will not be paused or interrupted again. But there is much yet to learn.

Preface

The contents of this book are based on a paper titled *The Religion of the Fathers* begun in 2020, and presented during a conference at Aravada Springs, NV on March 27, 2021. Significant oral comments made during the presentation were recorded and then added to the text, which was then edited and prepared for this volume.

In order to talk about this subject, it was necessary to use content in the Book of Abraham, which has been under assault by critics for a long time. I was satisfied about the reliability, authenticity, and scriptural value of the Book of Abraham long ago, but after being satisfied, I quit buying and reading the exchange that has gone back and forth between critics and defenders. When this subject became something that I intended to address, I thought it appropriate to review the last eight years' worth of material to catch up on the give-and-take arguments between the two sides. I had to buy a new "last-eight-years" library to supplement my Book of Abraham materials.

I've undertaken this effort to show the courtesy to the partisans of being informed about the ongoing arguments for and against the Book of Abraham. I've done the homework, and let both the polemicists and the apologists inform me. I've read the materials cited in the footnotes and much more, and have paid attention to the ongoing dialogue.

I think the overwhelming majority of the dialogue invested in the give-and-take about the Book of Abraham is completely off-point and has no value in trying to determine the authenticity of the book.

The gifts of God are almost entirely incapable of being transferred from one to another. Each person has to come to God on their own. Oliver Cowdery was a man of faith, and he believed in Christ and the possibility of the second coming of Christ being in close proximity to his lifetime. He believed in, and he got answers from, God; and when he heard about Joseph, he went to volunteer to become his scribe.

One of the early revelations given to Oliver talked about Oliver's gift which permitted him to get "yes" or "no" answers from God. Oliver used what we would call a "divining rod" (a stick) that would respond positively or negatively. The revelation calls it a "gift." It may seem like a peculiar gift to you and I; but it was, nevertheless, a gift, and it came from God.

Joseph had a gift in which he was capable of receiving revelation— sometimes through instruments, sometimes by study, sometimes by God speaking through him in the first person spontaneously. How that happened was unique to him. The way in which you relate to God is unique to you.

Those who would like to anchor Joseph's restoring the Book of Abraham to the surviving Joseph Smith papyri fragment, and claim it is the sole source for the Book of Abraham neglect the bigger part of the process. The inspiration or revelation from God is the much greater part of the process.

Consider how varied the ways answers come from God: Can God use a bird in flight to answer a prayer? Can God use a billboard to convey a truth or an idea? Can God use a song to inspire you? Can God use the words of a poet, speaking about something entirely different, to convey to the mind, inspired by the light of Heaven, to provide words that speak directly and immediately to answer you?

There's a chorus in one of the Indigo Girls' songs:

> I spent four years prostrate to the higher mind
> Got my paper and I was free
> I went to the doctor, I went to the mountains
> I looked to the children, I drank from the fountains
> There's more than one answer to these questions pointing me in a crooked line
> And the less I seek my source for some definitive
> Closer I am to fine (*Closer to Fine*, Indigo Girls)

It's a beautiful song. It's about frustration with gurus, generally, and the notion you need to divorce yourself from them, because the answers from most of the purportedly authoritative sources will always point you in a crooked line. Only the paths of God are straight.

In one of the very earliest recorded meetings in Kirtland, Ohio, Hyrum Smith introduced his brother, Joseph, and said that Joseph would explain to the audience the process by which the Book of Mormon was translated. Joseph declined and said, 'It's not needful for that to be explained.' The person who understood the process of translating the Book of Mormon was Joseph Smith. Even the scribes who were in the immediate area don't know the process by which the Book of Mormon was translated.

The reason critics of the Book of Abraham attack it is to attack Joseph Smith. Those who want to discredit Joseph go at the Book of Abraham to then extend the argument from the translation of the papyri to the translation of the Book of Mormon. They want to dismiss the work of Joseph Smith altogether and not have to trouble themselves with the heavy, unnerving obligation that devolves upon the shoulders of every person who finds out that God sent a prophet (in the form of Joseph Smith) in order to begin anew and complete the process of preparing mankind for the second coming of the Lord.

And so, criticisms directed at the Book of Abraham and that translation process use it as a surrogate for criticism, ultimately, aimed at the Book of Mormon—in order that Joseph might be diminished as an authoritative figure, on the one hand, and to dismiss him as an authoritative figure, on the other hand.

Well, if you start with the real proposition about the Book of Abraham (which is where we ought to go first), that is: Is Joseph Smith the kind of man that would be capable of receiving a revelation going back to the era of Abraham to restore an ancient text? Is Joseph Smith capable of doing that? Or is he a craven manipulator who's dishonest, inventive, fanciful, egomaniacal, and in it for his own self-gain? That's the real question that the 'Book of Abraham translation issues' raises.

And for the answer to that question, I don't think you can parse your way through a relic of papyri—which is clearly only a fragment of what he was working with, and doesn't match the description of the text. What was translated by Joseph was in a beautiful hand in both red and black ink [from a letter Oliver Cowdery sent to William Frye, dated December 25, 1835, and published in the *Latter Day Saints' Messenger and Advocate* of the same month]. The fragment we have is in black ink, there's no red ink, and it is quite sloppy.

I don't think we should let Joseph Smith off the hook for being accountable and responsible for being a virtuous man, a truthful man, and a reliable man. But I don't think you answer those questions by an appeal to a fragment of papyri and what modern Egyptologists may be able to divine from a complex language that had migrated from hieroglyph to hieratic to demotic—and that, too, over five millennia of time.

Abraham is believed to have lived during the first Intermediate Period of Egypt. The Joseph Smith papyri fragments were created in the Greco-Roman era, about eighteen dynasties later, after the influence of the Greco-Roman world. The Book of Breathings and the text from which it was drawn – the Book of the Dead – are very, very late Egyptian documents. There is nothing comparable to it in an existing culture—maybe in China; maybe if you go to Hong Kong, and you walk down the street in Hong Kong, and you take a look at all the advertisements that are on the billboards that are in both English and Mandarin or Cantonese; and use that as the measure of reconstructing something from one of the earliest Chinese dynasties, maybe that would be akin to what Egyptologists are attempting. There was no McDonald's back then so it would hardly work. It would be trying to bridge a gulf that is unimaginably foreign.

The earliest pictographic representations were done alongside a story. Both the pictographic representation, and the story told you what the picture was about. Could the picture be used to tell yet another story by making a few minor changes and then tell a different story? The answer to that is (obviously) "yes," you could. It would not be until after you insert additional commentary designed to explain how the picture fit the new story that it would make sense. That would not mean the representation did not borrow from another account, or an earlier account, or a different account, and then been modified and adapted to tell another story, all while using the same pictographic writing.

Joseph was like a sponge when he thought he could get truth or help from others, and he was meek and humble in that respect. But if God had revealed something to him, he was an iron-fisted, immovable man for the truth, personally and privately, just as the scriptures say concerning Moses. Moses was the meekest of all men. If you just read the statements of Moses (in Exodus), you will find meekness in that man. If you will read Joseph Smith's three documents in A Man Without Doubt, you will also see a meek man— unbelievably frustrated by some of the circumstances of his life, searching to find the right way out of the dilemmas, trying to get

God aroused to anger in the same way that the circumstances aroused Joseph to anger, but always submitting to the will of God. Joseph Smith went to Carthage, knowing (or at least expecting) he would not come back—and commenting that if his life was of no value to his friends he would willingly die.

Say what you want about those final moments in the life of Joseph Smith. He put himself in harm's way to prove his faithfulness to his friends. He would not forsake them (as they claimed he was doing in their hour of need) and ultimately gave up his life. That is not the conduct of a con-man. That is not the behavior of a liar, cheat, thief or immoral conman. Joseph, in my view, was not just a virtuous man, but one who "hath no greater love," because he surrendered his life at the behest of his brethren—in part with the hope that by losing his life, Nauvoo would be spared the slaughter that happened earlier at Far West, and Haun's Mill, and elsewhere.

When we consider the translation issues and controversy about the Book of Abraham, the real issue is: However the mind of Joseph was set on fire with the restoration text of father Abraham's account of his search, the resulting text is either from heaven or it is a lie.

There was a book series (now abandoned) begun at Brigham Young University.[1] The first volume of which was pretty good. It took unique concepts from the Book of Abraham which were unknown in the Christian world when the Book of Abraham was first published, examining only unique ideas from the Book of Abraham (about which Joseph Smith would have known nothing), and compared those to other materials from diverse places, including legends or ancient stories about the life of Abraham. There were Hindu traditions about Abraham that preserved some of the very same things found in the Book of Abraham. There were Islamic texts and also Coptic Egyptian texts, and others that mirror the Book of Abraham. These stories were amalgamated into one volume to show just how much Joseph Smith hit the bullseye with the Book of Abraham.

That approach does not defend Joseph Smith as a translator of Egyptian, because it has nothing to do with the papyri. But it does a

---

[1] *Traditions about the Early Life of Abraham* (Volume 1) by John A. Tvedtnes (Editor), Brian M. Hauglid (Editor), and John Gee (Editor); Brigham Young University; 74th ed. edition (April 1, 2005).

good job of defending Joseph Smith as a revelator, as someone to whom God could reveal light and truth and he could accurately record it–because echoes of the unique material in the Book of Abraham show up in the ancient world and in other cultures that date back to the time of Abraham.

So, the real question is: Do you trust Joseph?

Denver C. Snuffer, Jr.
June 1, 2021

Prologue

As the Restoration continues to roll out, more and more of its teachings, commandments, rights, privileges, and honors will become public. This will create a growing contrast between the darkness of the world, failed institutions, and ambitious pretenders. There is no end of grandiose claims and institutional promises, but falsehoods become apparent when compared with light and truth from God.[2] False claims and false revelation contradict Scripture. The proliferation of "sealed Book of Mormon" texts[3] is contrary to the Book of Mormon promises about the timing of it coming forth.[4] Likewise, attempting to now practice the United Order violates God's will since Joseph Smith rescinded it on March 6, 1840. Joseph prophesied any attempt at present will prove "a perfect abortion."[5] Ignorance damns people, and the effort to get light and truth requires study, obedience, prayer, and revelation from God.

---

[2] Obvious mistakes such as misnaming angels ("Moroni" instead of "Nephi") or claiming the angel "Raphael" visited a person is an unmistakable sign of mere pretense—or worse, deception. Raphael has a limited earthly role (see T&C 151:15 and 157:31), never accompanying and lingering here. His role is heavenly until the Second Coming (see Judas 1:3 [Jude 1:14-15]). All citations in this book are to the Restoration Edition of Scripture, available to read online at www.scriptures.info or for purchase through www.scriptures.shop. LDS citations are provided secondarily in square brackets.

[3] Nemelka (claiming to be the reincarnated Hyrum Smith), Berger (implying himself to be the reincarnated Joseph Smith), the Mentinah Archives, and a new fellow named Ackerman all purport to have the sealed Book of Mormon plates.

[4] See Ether 1:17 [4:3-7]. There is little doubt the Gentiles have not and do not exhibit faith akin to the Brother of Jared.

[5] "He said that the Law of consecration could not be kept here, & that it was the will of the Lord that we should desist from trying to keep it, & if persisted in it would produce a perfect abortion, & that he assumed the whole responsibility of not keeping it untill proposed by himself" (*Joseph Smith Papers* [hereafter JSP], *Documents, Volume 7*, p. 215, all spelling as in original).

Context for the Book of Abraham
Part 1

The name "Jesus Christ" is Greek. An Anglicized Hebrew version of that name is "Joshua the Messiah" or, more phonetically correct, "Yeshua the Mashiach." God promised Adam there would be a Messiah or Christ sent to save his (Adam's) descendants. Angels preached the gospel of the promised Messiah to righteous men and women beginning with Father Adam. Abraham was taught that same gospel.[6] Jesus the Messiah was born in Bethlehem, lived as a mortal, and fulfilled God's Messianic promises. He was not an innovator. Instead, He restored that gospel originally revealed to the Patriarchal Fathers.

This book is about understanding the worship of our Messiah. An 1833 revelation promised further information to be given to the faithful who obeyed God's commandments:

> *I give unto you these sayings that you may understand and know* **how** *to worship, and know* **what** *you worship, that you may come unto the Father in my name, and in due time receive of his fullness, for if you keep my commandments, you shall receive of his fullness and be glorified in me as I am glorified in the Father. Therefore, I say unto you, you shall receive grace for grace.* (T&C 93:7 [D&C 93:19-20], emphasis added)

A prophecy of Malachi is recorded in every volume of Scripture: Old Covenants, New Covenants, Book of Mormon, and Teachings and Commandments. The prophecy promises that before the great and dreadful day of the Lord the hearts of the children will turn to the Fathers or (as stated in the JST Old Covenants): *Behold, I will send you Elijah the prophet before the coming of the great and dreadful day of the Lord. And he shall* **seal** *the heart of the Fathers to the children and the heart of the children to their Fathers, lest I come and smite the earth with a curse* (Malachi 1:12 [4:5-6], emphasis added).[7]

---

[6] "And the scripture, foreseeing that God would justify the heathen through faith, preached before the gospel unto Abraham" (Galatians 1:7 [3:8]).

[7] In the Book of Mormon, Christ renders it: "Behold, I will send you Elijah the prophet before the coming of the great and dreadful day of the Lord, and he shall turn the heart of the fathers to the children and the heart of the children to their fathers, lest I come and smite the earth with a curse" (3 Nephi 11:5 [25:5-6]).

Nephi quoted it to Joseph Smith a little differently: *And he shall plant in the hearts of the children the promises made to the fathers, and the hearts of the children shall* **turn** *to their fathers; if it were not so, the whole earth would be* **utterly wasted** *at his coming* (Joseph Smith History [hereafter JSH] 3:4, [1:39], emphasis added).

Two versions of Malachi's prophecy have the very same interesting wording. Both the Old Covenants and the Book of Mormon twice use the word "heart" in the singular,[8] but "fathers" and "children" are plural. It is a small change but an important and revealing one. The Fathers are of **one heart**, and to the extent there are to be children sealed to them, the children will also be of one (and the same) heart.

In this book, I hope to clarify and identify who the "fathers" are. It is not your immediate ancestors from the last 20 or so generations;[9] all of them who died without the required knowledge and acceptance of fullness of the gospel are in spirit prison. They are, therefore, damned[10] and cannot progress until preparations are made[11] to improve their resurrection.[12]

Our hearts must become one. United hearts seem to be in a distant latitude from where we are now. Even then, before any attempt at "sealing" begins, the first question is the identity of the "fathers" to whom our singular heart must be sealed to avoid being "cursed" or, as Christ warned, "utterly wasted at his coming."

There is a **true** religion, and it was revealed first to Adam. Adam not only received and practiced that true religion, it is through him that every subsequent dispensation of the gospel has been revealed. Joseph Smith taught:

---

[8] The Book of Mormon account of Malachi is provided by Christ in 3 Nephi 11:1-5 [23:14-25:6]. Since it is "the most correct of any book on earth," according to Joseph Smith, the wording of the Malachi prophecy found there would be the most correct.

[9] See, e.g., *The Mission of Elijah Reconsidered*, beginning at p. 27; reprinted in *Essays: Three Degrees*, beginning at p. 109.

[10] Using the term "damned" as it is defined in the Glossary of the T&C: "To cease progressing or to regress. Damnation merely means the end of progress. So when one fails to progress in understanding, he voluntarily damns himself. ... Damnation means hedging up the way so that one cannot progress" (citations omitted).

[11] See T&C 151:6. Note this preparation requires the ability to "bind" (or seal) on Earth to have it recognized in Heaven.

[12] See T&C 122:5 [D&C 137:7-9].

> *Commencing with Adam, who was the first man, who is spoken of in Daniel as being the Ancient of Days, or in other words, the first and oldest of all, the great grand progenitor, of whom it is said in another place, He is Michael, because he was the first and father of all, not only by progeny, but he was the first to hold the spiritual blessings, to whom was made known the plan of ordinances for the salvation of his posterity unto the end, and to whom Christ was first revealed, and through whom Christ **has been** revealed from Heaven and will continue **to be** revealed from henceforth. **Adam** holds the keys of the dispensation of the fullness of times; i.e., the dispensation of all the times have been and will be revealed through him, from the beginning to Christ, and from Christ to the end of all the dispensations that are to be revealed.*
>
> *...that all things pertaining to that dispensation should be conducted precisely in accordance with the preceding dispensations. And again, God purposed in himself that there should not be an Eternal fullness until every dispensation should be fulfilled and gathered together in one, and that all things whatever that should be gathered together in one, in those dispensations, unto the same fullness and Eternal glory, should be in Christ Jesus.*
>
> *Therefore, he set the ordinances to be the same for ever and ever, and set Adam to watch over them, to reveal them from Heaven to man or to send angels to reveal them.* (T&C 140:3,5-6; emphasis added)

God gave to Adam the right of "dominion" over the Earth and everything (correspondingly, **everyone**) on the Earth.[13] That was part of the original true religion.[14] When the true religion was combined with the right to hold dominion or preside as a High

---

[13] See Genesis 2:8-9 [1:26-28]. The word "dominion" and the word "domicile" come from the same root. A domicile is a place set in order and arranged, planted with a yard and garden, and everyone and everything has a place for occupancy—something made beautiful and aesthetic by the effort (or husbandry) of the residents. That image of "husbandman over a domicile" was what God conferred on Adam when he was given dominion over the entire Creation. So Adam (and his posterity) were charged to do something much different with this Creation than what mankind has done. We rather brutalize it into submission. We are more vandals and raiders than husbandmen to the Earth.

[14] Cain aspired to Adam's status of holding dominion at the head of the human family. This ambition fueled his jealousy and, ultimately, his murder of Abel. Cain did not consider murdering Adam, because he respected Adam's position. He honored his father's right, envied it, and needed for it to be respected by others for his own ambition to succeed. Cain was willing to assassinate the heir but not the holder. He did not want any holder (hopefully himself) to be in peril of assassination.

Priest, it was called the "Holy Order after the Order of the Son of God."[15] This was shortened to "Holy Order."[16] It has also been called the Melchizedek Priesthood.[17] Because of the too frequent use of the term "Melchizedek Priesthood" by the LDS Church and resulting confusion about the meaning of the term, I have redefined "priesthood" and avoid making use of that term without clarification.[18] In this book, the term "Holy Order" is used to mean the original priestly position conferred on Adam and thereafter passed on to the one eldest, worthy descendant in each subsequent generation. The religion then taught by him was correct and held salvation.

The Patriarchal Fathers are Adam, Seth, Enos, Cainan, Mahalalel, Jared, Enoch, Methuselah, Lamech, Noah, Shem/Melchizedek, Abraham, Isaac, Jacob, and Joseph.[19] These 15 generational heads stood, like Adam, as God's Patriarchal Father and High Priest at the head of God's family on Earth. There were many others who believed in the religion taught by Adam and the Patriarchal Fathers, but the Holy Order given to Adam was always held in its fullness by the eldest worthy descendant in each subsequent generation until–skipping generations to–Abraham.[20]

---

[15] See Alma 9:10 [13:1-9]; also T&C 140:2.

[16] See, e.g., 2 Nephi 5:1 [6:2]; Alma 3:10 [5:53]; 6:2 [8:4]; 10:1 [13:10-16]; 20:1 [43:2]; 21:42 [49:30]; and Ether 5:2 [12:6-12], among other places. The Holy Order was lost to Israel at the time of Moses, and a lesser Aaronic Priesthood was established. "I will take away the Priesthood out of their midst. Therefore, my Holy Order and the ordinances thereof shall not go before them, for my presence shall not go up in their midst lest I destroy them" (Exodus 18:5 [JST 34:1]). "Therefore, he took Moses out of their midst, and the Holy Priesthood also. And the lesser priesthood continued, which priesthood holds the key of the ministering of angels, and the preparatory gospel, which gospel is the gospel of repentance, and of baptism, and the remission of sins, and the law of carnal commandments, which the Lord in his wrath caused to continue with the house of Aaron, among the children of Israel, until John, whom God raised up" (T&C 82:14 [D&C 84:25-27]).

[17] See T&C 141:41 [D&C 124:123].

[18] This subject was discussed in greater detail in the Orem talk entitled "Priesthood" and transcribed with footnotes into the paper "Priesthood, Lecture 5, Orem, Utah," which is available as a download from www.denversnuffer.com. The paper helps clarify the subject, and in particular, page 29 is where a new definition is proposed. The paper was the basis for the chapter on "Priesthood" in *Preserving the Restoration* (Mill Creek Press, 2015).

[19] Ephraim also received the birthright from Jacob/Israel (see Genesis 12:18 [48:8-22]). However, unlike the others, we have no significant account of him serving in that role. His father, Joseph, was the last in the line to clearly occupy the Holy Order.

[20] As Abraham described the order, "It came down from the Fathers, from the beginning of time, yea, even from the beginning (or before the foundations of the earth) to the present time, even the right of the firstborn (or the first man–who is Adam–or first father) through the Fathers unto me"(Abraham 1:1 [1:3]).

Abraham was the first precedent for "sealing" into the Order, tying a descendant separated by generations into the position of patriarchal successor to Shem/Melchizedek. This precedent helps explain Joseph Smith's later practice of sealing others to him. Given the examples of Abraham and Joseph Smith, it becomes clear that the Holy Order does not have to be exclusively dynastic (passing in one family line) but can branch out to include any other worthy member of the line, however distant or separated by generations.

The Patriarchal head of the Holy Order is the shepherd for the faithful, husbandman for the Creation, and teacher responsible for dispensing Divine knowledge.[21] It is more than competent gospel teaching; it is authoritatively dispensing a message from a position established and recognized by God, hence Joseph Smith's observation that *there are many teachers, but perhaps not many fathers* (T&C 139:12). When the Holy Order is active, these obligations attach to the position in every generation.

The first or Patriarchal Fathers learned the true religion from Adam and practiced it under his direction. Adam taught the first eight patriarchs born after him.[22] Their religion was Adam's religion, and their understanding reached back to the Garden of Eden.[23]

The majority of Adam's family abandoned the truth. From the time of Adam, most people who have been given the opportunity to receive the gospel in their respective dispensations have dwindled in unbelief. The Book of Mormon repeatedly describes people dwindling in unbelief. An angel foretold to Nephi (the first prophet-writer in the first book of the Book of Mormon) that all his

---

[21] In later dispensations, the roles have been divided: for example, separating the prophetic-teaching role from the kingly-government role. This was the case with the brother of Jared (prophet) and Jared (king). Nephi also divided the teaching-prophet role from the kingship. These separate roles are also evident when King David was condemned by the prophet Nathan for the murder of Uriah (see 2 Samuel 4:11-13 [12:1-12]). "Although David was a king, he never did obtain the spirit and power of Elijah and the fullness of the Priesthood..." (*Teachings of the Prophet Joseph Smith* [hereafter *TPJS*], p. 339). The Holy Order, however, when held in its fullness, combines together the prophet-priest-and-king. That authority must be restored to the Earth and then voluntarily returned to the Messiah before the Second Coming to fulfill the plan ordained before the foundation of the world.

[22] These included Seth, Enos, Cainan, Mahalalel, Jared, Enoch, Methuselah, and Lamech.

[23] "The Ancient Egyptians also spoke of a mythical epoch known as *sep tepi*, the First Time, seen as a kind of golden age..." (Andrew Collins, *Gods of Eden*, Bear & Company, Vermont [2002], p. 6).

descendants and his brothers' descendants would dwindle in unbelief.[24]

Dwindling happens whenever light and truth are neglected, forgotten, or rejected. The term "unbelief" applies not when people cease believing, but when they hold false beliefs. Those false beliefs include incomplete, unfinished, or incorrect ideas. Unbelief comes as much from rejecting Scripture[25] as from deleting or changing ordinances.[26]

The truth has dwindled, and there are not accurate enough Scriptures available to know all that has been lost. Upheavals in history have produced a barrier keeping the first religion away from us. Margaret Barker has spent a lifetime studying ancient Israel, largely pursuing the First Temple religion of Israel. Her goal is modest. She is trying to reconstruct the Old Testament era from Solomon to Ezra. We are trying to reach back to Adam. Even with her more modest aim, she has concluded it is impossible for us to know what really took place. She calls the present state of all our understanding nothing more than "supposition":

> The exile in Babylon is a formidable barrier to anyone wanting to reconstruct the religious beliefs and practices of ancient Jerusalem. If we are to discover any possible reason for the distinction between the sons of El/Elyon and the sons of Yahweh it is a barrier, which has to be acknowledged. Enormous developments took place in the wake of enormous destruction, and these two factors make certainty quite impossible. They make *all* certainty impossible, and this too must be acknowledged, for the customary descriptions of ancient Israel's religion are themselves no more than supposition.[27]

---

[24] See 1 Nephi 3:18 [12:19-23].
[25] "Woe unto you lawyers, for you have taken away the key of knowledge, the fullness of the scriptures. You enter not in yourselves into the kingdom, and those who were entering in, you hindered" (Luke 8:17 [11:52]).
[26] "The earth also is defiled under the inhabitants thereof, because they have transgressed the laws, changed the ordinance, broken the everlasting covenant" (Isaiah 7:1 [24:5]).
[27] Margaret Barker, *The Great Angel: A Study of Israel's Second God*, Westminster John Knox Press (1992), p. 12, citations omitted, italics in original.

Belief is only possible by receiving the truth.²⁸ It is important to have the truth in order to acquire belief. The Lord commanded Joseph Smith to revise the Bible in order to permit "belief" (or "correct understanding"). One of the corrections Joseph made was to the exchange between Jesus and the lawyers. Luke was revised to now read: *Woe unto you lawyers, for you have taken away the key of knowledge, the fullness of the scriptures. You enter not in yourselves into the kingdom, and those who were entering in, you hindered* (Luke 8:17 [11:52]). Without the "fullness of the scriptures," it is impossible to have belief. Truth is the key of knowledge.

Joseph Smith's revision of the Bible was designed to restore the Bible to read: *...even as they are in [God's] own bosom, to the salvation of [God's] elect* (T&C 18:6 [D&C 35:20]). From the command to commence the corrected Bible project until the command to publish it, Joseph's inspired revision was referred to in 14 revelations.²⁹ The revised Bible was quoted exclusively in Lectures on Faith.³⁰ The Bible revision was essential for people to have belief. Without it, the saints would dwindle in unbelief because they lacked the truths God intended to be known and accepted by His followers. Joseph Smith knew this and warned about how crucial it was for the revised Bible (which he called the "fullness of the scriptures") to be published for believers. In an October 1831 Conference, he taught the saints: "God had often sealed up the Heavens because of covetousness in the church. Said the Lord would cut his work short in righteousness and except the church receive the fullness of the scriptures they would yet fall."³¹

The fullness of the Scriptures was never published in Joseph Smith's lifetime—or **ever** by **any church**. The RLDS Church published an incomplete and altered version that excluded revisions made by Joseph Smith and included revisions made by a committee. A significant part of the work accomplished by Joseph Smith has been neglected by the LDS or altered by the RLDS (now the Community of Christ), and both of those groups have dwindled in unbelief. Because they have incomplete Scriptures, having rejected part of

---

[28] Belief is defined in the Glossary to mean: "Understanding and accepting true doctrine (*see* 3 Nephi 7:4)."
[29] See T&C 18:6 [D&C 35:20]; 20:1 [37:1-2]; 26:5 [42:12-17]; 31:13 [45:60-63]; 66:2 [73:3-6]; 69:3 [76:11-17]; 76:2; 88:1; 90:4 [90:12-18]; 91:1 [91]; 93:17 [93:52-53]; 97:3 [94:10-12]; 105:13 [104:54-59]; 141:31 [124:88-90].
[30] See, e.g., Lectures on Faith 2:5,10,22-24,26,37; 3:1, among many others.
[31] JSP, Documents, Volume 2: July 1831 – January 1833, p. 85.

what the Lord has as "scriptures in His own bosom,"[32] it cannot be otherwise. All of the break-off groups that have separated from the LDS or the RLDS have similarly dwindled in unbelief.

The Restoration has not been able to advance until recently when a penitent group of believers repented and endeavored to recover and reclaim what was discarded. In the inspired "Prayer for Covenant," these past failures are acknowledged, and the Lord was asked to accept our repentance. Here are some excerpts from that prayer:

> We are mindful that in 1832 the gentile saints were condemned for vanity and unbelief because they treated lightly the things they had received, and they were warned by you that they would remain under condemnation until they repent and remember the new covenant, even the Book of Mormon and the former commandments, not only to say, but to do. You commanded the gentiles that they bring forth fruit meet for their Father's kingdom, and if they failed to do so, there remained a scourge and judgment to be poured out upon those who claimed to be the children of Zion. They failed to bring forth the required fruit, and were judged and scourged, and then violently driven out of Jackson County, Missouri.

> ...Even today the gentile saints justify lying to others as part of their religion, believing you will vindicate them in their dishonesty. They seek deep to hide their counsel from others, and now deny your judgments against their ancestors, claiming you have never rejected them. They have, as you foretold, spoken both good and evil of your prophet Joseph. They ascribe many of their wicked practices to Joseph, who correctly told their ancestors that **they never knew him** – for indeed, the gentile saints have grown distant from you because of their willful rebellion, pride, foolishness, and blindness. We acknowledge that we must distinguish ourselves from them, admit the errors of the past, and in the depths of humility, seek to be reclaimed as yours.

> The neglect and rebellion of the saints during Joseph's day and thereafter included how they have treated the scriptures, carelessly inserting numerous errors and transcription problems into the Book of Mormon and other commandments and revelations. The original Book of Mormon translation manuscript was placed in the cornerstone of the Nauvoo House where water and mold destroyed over 70% of the text. This was a similitude to the restoration provided

---

[32] See T&C 18:6 [D&C 35:20].

by you through Joseph. Just as the original manuscript was allowed to decay, with only approximately 28% surviving, so likewise the Restoration has also decayed.

...The other revelations given through Joseph Smith have also not been maintained and transmitted to us in their purity.

*...We ask to be corrected in anything we have gathered and ask to be instructed by you to discard what ought to be discarded, and inspired to keep only those things which should be kept. We were not responsible for neglecting your warnings, for treating lightly the Book of Mormon and former commandments, nor for failing to do as you asked, but **have inherited** that legacy and acknowledge that we also suffer under your condemnation as our inheritance.*

...Though only a remnant of the original faith you established through Joseph has likewise survived, we ask to be reconnected as a people to you by covenant, to make us yours, connected to a living vine, restored as a people, and numbered with Israel. We seek as a people to honor you and to keep your commandments so that a living body of your disciples may again exist on the earth. We desire that we may rise up through your grace and mercy so that you will perform your oath and vindicate your promises to the fathers concerning a faithful latter-day body of gentiles to be numbered with the remnant of Jacob, that your kingdom may come and your will be done on earth as it is in Heaven.

...We ask that you accept these books as yours so that people of faith may then rely upon this work as your word to this generation, as a standard for governing ourselves, as a law, and as a covenant, to establish a rule for our faith, and as the expression of our religion, so we may have correct faith and be enabled to worship you in truth. If this body of writings are not acceptable, we ask that you guide us further so we may correct, remove, or add whatever you would require for the writings to become acceptable for a covenant and law, a rule of faith, as a correct expression of the religion that honors you, so we may be in possession of correct faith and be enabled to worship you in truth. (T&C 156:2,7-8,10-11,15,17; emphasis added)

The prayer and the effort to recover the fullness of the Scriptures pleased the Lord. He answered by commending the recovery and accepting the Scriptures. His "Answer to the Prayer for Covenant" states, in part:

We asked the Lord to tell us if something ought to be deleted and to tell us if something ought to be added, and He did both of those things. Things were deleted and things then were added in response to the prayer. But His answer included these:

> *The records in the form you have of the Old Covenants, given from Adam until Moses and from Moses to John, are of great worth and can serve my purposes, and are acceptable for this time.*
>
> *The records of my apostles containing my New Covenants were to contain the fullness of my gospel, but during the formation of the great and abominable church, many parts were discarded and other parts were altered. False brethren who did not fear me intended to corrupt and to pervert the right way, to blind the eyes and harden the hearts of others, in order to obtain power and authority over them.*
>
> *Conspiracies have corrupted the records, beginning among the Jews, and again following the time of my apostles, and yet again following the time of Joseph and Hyrum. As you have labored with the records you have witnessed the alterations and insertions, and your effort to recover them pleases me and is of great worth.* (T&C 157:13-15)

Ours are the only Scriptures approved by God as *sufficient for the labor now underway* (T&C 177:2). However, the Lord stopped short of endorsing them as without flaws.

> *The records you have gathered as scriptures yet lack many of my words, have errors throughout, and contain things that are not of me, because the records you used in your labors have not been maintained nor guarded against the cunning plans of false brethren who have been deceived by Satan.* (T&C 157:12)

The Lord explained:

> *What you have gathered as scriptures are acceptable to me for this time and contain many plain and precious things. Nevertheless, whoso is enlightened by the spirit shall obtain the greater benefit, because you need not think they contain all my words nor that more will not be given, for there are many things yet to be restored unto my people.*
>
> *...There will yet be records restored from all the tribes, that will be gathered again into one, and also as I have said, there is some truth in*

> *the Apocrypha, including the Pseudepigrapha and scrolls recovered at Nag Hammadi, and other New Testament texts uncovered since the time of Joseph Smith, and findings at Qumran, and there are other records yet to be recovered; and whoso is enlightened by the spirit shall obtain benefit by their careful study.* (Ibid. vs. 44,47)

We have the best available, but they are to be understood through the power of the spirit. In another revelation, the Lord explained this about our Scriptures:

> *These scriptures are sent forth to be my warning to the world, my comfort to the faithful, my counsel to the meek, my reproof to the proud, my rebuke to the contentious, and my condemnation of the wicked. They are my invitation to all mankind to flee from corruption, repent and be baptized in my name, and prepare for the coming judgment.*[33] (T&C 177:3)

Our Scriptures will do no good if they are not read or studied. We, like all other Restoration churches and groups, can also dwindle in unbelief.

Unlike the many existing and past Restoration believers, we must fight against falling into unbelief. Nephi warned us about the churches of the Restoration:

> *Yea, they have all gone out of the way, they have become corrupted; because of pride, and because of false teachers, and false doctrine, their churches have become corrupted, and their churches are lifted up; because of pride, they are puffed up. They rob the poor because of their fine sanctuaries; they rob the poor because of their fine clothing, and they persecute the meek and the poor in heart because in their pride they are puffed up. They wear stiff necks and high heads, yea, and because of pride, and wickedness, and abominations, and whoredoms, they have **all** gone astray, save it be a few who are the humble followers of Christ. Nevertheless, they are led, that in many instances they do err because they are taught by the precepts of men.* (2 Nephi 12:2 [11:8-14], emphasis added)[34]

---

[33] This final sentence of T&C 177:3 (as quoted here) was not part of the paper but was quoted during the talk.

[34] This can only mean the Restoration congregations—because no Catholic or Protestant churches would read the Book of Mormon, nor would Jewish, Islamic, Buddhist, or Hindu bodies read this warning. Its target audience are only those who have the Book of Mormon as part of their canon of Scripture.

We have no fine sanctuaries, and until commanded and instructed to do so, we do not anticipate building anything other than a single temple. We do not rob the poor, because our tithes are used only to aid the poor. We do not regard one above another, and we have no hierarchy in position to lead anyone astray. Nevertheless, we can still be proud, rob the poor by our overindulgence, and participate in abominations and whoredoms. Some foolish people among us have done these things. They must repent, or they cannot be gathered.

We have little reason to be unguarded. We can fail to study the recovered Scriptures approved by the Lord as a standard to govern our daily walk. We can fail to accept the obligations established by the Book of Mormon as a covenant and to use the Scriptures to correct ourselves and guide our words, thoughts, and deeds.[35] We can let the lusts of the flesh to control us. And when we do, we choose to dwindle in unbelief.

You have the new Scriptures. The leather-bound copies will shortly be distributed. Use them. Study them. Show appreciation to the Lord by refusing to dwindle in unbelief.

Joseph Smith was able to revise the Bible through God's inspiration.[36] It is important to prize the corrected Bible and do better than the saints of Joseph's day.

Despite nearly universal apostasy and rebellion against God **while Adam lived**, the line of the Patriarchal Fathers preserved the true religion. Noah had a father who knew and was taught by Adam. Noah's living grandfather, great-grandfather, and ancestors for

---

[35] See T&C 158:3.

[36] Following the baptism of both Joseph and Oliver Cowdery, Joseph reported, "Our minds being now enlightened, we began to have the scriptures laid open to our understandings, and the true meaning and intention of their more mysterious passages revealed unto us in a manner which we never could attain to previously, nor ever before had thought of" (JSH 14:4 [JS-H 1:74]). It was this enlightenment, inspired by the Spirit, that led to the Bible revision—not a commentary written by Adam Clarke. For a refutation of the accusation that Joseph Smith plagiarized Clarke, see Kent P. Jackson, "Some Notes on Joseph Smith and Adam Clarke," *Interpreter: A Journal of Latter-day Saint Faith and Scholarship*, Volume 40, 2020, pp. 15-60.

seven generations³⁷ also knew and were taught by Adam. Learning about God from His messengers and priests was (and still is) necessary to avoid dwindling in unbelief and falling into apostasy. The "angels" who ministered included mortals who were given Divine knowledge to teach.³⁸

Noah preserved the original religion of God through the cataclysm of the flood. Three of the sons of Noah were taught it, and Noah's most faithful son inherited the right. The fullness of the Holy Order was conferred upon Shem (who received the title "Melchizedek"³⁹). A descendant of Ham falsely claimed he held the Holy Order, but he could only institute an imitation of the Order.⁴⁰

After Melchizedek, an apostasy lasted until Abraham. Although he was raised by an idolater and lamented that his fathers offered sacrifices to idols,⁴¹ Abraham searched for the true God of Heaven.⁴² Abraham found God, and the covenant of the first Fathers was renewed and conferred upon him by Melchizedek.⁴³ Generations of apostates were excluded from the Holy Order, but Abraham was adopted into the line by Melchizedek, thereby restoring continuity back to Adam.

---

37 Enoch was translated before Noah's birth; however, Enoch continued to minister as an angel to his mortal descendants following his ascent into heaven until the time of the deluge. He will return at Christ's Second Coming and minister again among Terrestrial beings living in the Millennium. "Now this Enoch, God reserved unto himself that he should not die at that time, and appointed unto him a ministry unto terrestrial bodies, of whom there has been but little revealed. He is reserved also unto the presidency of a dispensation, and more shall be said of him and terrestrial bodies in another treatise. He is a ministering angel, to minister to those who shall be heirs of salvation, and appeared unto Jude [Judas] as Abel did unto Paul. Therefore, Jude [Judas] spoke of him, 14th and 15th verses in Jude [Epistle of Judas 1:3]" (T&C 140:13). Therefore, Noah would have had access to his great-grandfather, Enoch, as a ministering angel.
38 "The belief that a human could be transformed into an angel when he experienced the presence of God is one of the characteristics of texts which retained the patterns of the royal cult. What had been the ascent of the king became the ascent of the mystic to contemplate the throne. The ascent transformed him" (Barker, *The Great Angel*, supra, p. 79; see also p. 121).
39 T&C Glossary entry for "Melchizedek" explains, "In 1844, the church-owned newspaper identified Shem as Melchizedek" (citing *Times & Seasons*, Vol. 5, p. 746, December 15, 1844). The new name meant "king" (Melek) and "righteous" (Zadok). In the Talmud *Nedarim* 32b and *Targum Neofiti*, Melchizedek is identified as Shem.
40 See Abraham 2:3 [1:25-27].
41 See Abraham 1:2 [1:5-7].
42 See Abraham 1:1 [1:1-4].
43 See Abraham 1:5 [1:15-19].

Abraham represents the key Patriarchal Father prophesied of in Malachi. Abraham not only renewed the covenant of "the fathers"[44] (including Noah[45] and Enoch[46]), but also, through the Abrahamic covenant, God established Abraham as the new head of the family of God on Earth.[47] God told Abraham: *As many as receive this gospel shall be called after your name and shall be accounted your seed, and shall rise up and bless you, as unto their Father* (Abraham 3:1 [2:10]). For us, connecting to Abraham is akin to the original Patriarchs' connection with Adam. Turning the heart of the children to the Fathers is a required part of the gospel, and after God's covenant with him, salvation for all subsequent generations is dependent on being accounted Abraham's seed.[48]

The covenant with Abraham was renewed with Isaac, who also became the Patriarchal head and husbandman-father of the faithful. Believers thereafter likewise are numbered as Isaac's "seed" through the renewal and extension of the covenant.[49] God renewed it again with Jacob.[50] The covenantal relationship of these three Patriarchs in three successive generations is the reason the Scriptures use "the God of Abraham, and of Isaac, and of Jacob" as one name for Deity.[51]

Accordingly, the more we can know of Abraham, the more we can know of the covenant with the Fathers spoken of by Malachi. Any book written by Abraham should be priceless to us.

The Book of Abraham translated by Joseph Smith has become a battleground because it is so important for our salvation. On one side are those who hope Joseph has made it possible to be sealed to the Fathers. Opposing them are those who cannot believe Joseph supplied a text of any value for salvation. The fight over the Book of

---

[44] Ibid.
[45] Ibid.
[46] See Genesis 7:11 [13:14-18].
[47] See Abraham 3:1 [2:10].
[48] Hence Isaiah's admonition: "Look unto the rock from which you were hewn, and to the hole of the pit from which you are dug. Look unto Abraham, your father, and unto Sarah that bore you; for I called him alone, and blessed him, and increased him" (Isaiah 18:2 [51:1-2]).
[49] See Genesis 7:33; 9:4 [17:19,21].
[50] See, e.g., Genesis 12:42 [JST 50:36]; Exodus 2:1 [2:24]; 4:1 [6:3]; Leviticus 13:15 [26:42]; Deuteronomy 3:11 [9:5]; Psalm 105:2 [105:5-10]; 1 Nephi 5:20 [17:40].
[51] See, e.g., Exodus 2:3,5 [3:6,15]; Matthew 10:22 [22:32]; Mark 5:43 [12:26]; Luke 12:10 [20:37]; Acts 2:2 [3:13]; 4:6 [7:32]; 1 Nephi 2:1 [6:4]; 5:36 [19:10]; Mosiah 11:3 [23:23]; Alma 17:1 [36:2]; 3 Nephi 2:14 [4:30].

Abraham is now aimed at the entire Restoration and Joseph's Divine calling. Because of the controversy, I need to address the authenticity of the Book of Abraham in order to discuss God's covenant with the Fathers.

There are several threads of thought to be drawn together. The first one involves understanding different eras of written language used at the time of Abraham.

Most scholars believe Abraham lived around 2100 BC, during the 9th Dynasty of Egypt.[52] Moses lived around 1400 BC. Moses lived 700 years later. Egyptian texts date back to before 3400 BC. A written Hebrew language was not developed until 900 BC, a half-millennium after Moses. Accordingly, since Moses composed the first five books of the Old Covenants, he would have used Egyptian characters. Hence, the Scriptures written on the plates of brass recovered from Laban and used by the Nephites were written in Egyptian.[53]

The Hebrew language developed as a spoken language first, and a written language was added sometime later. The Book of Mormon confirms that although the Nephites spoke Hebrew, they used Egyptian characters to write their records. As Moroni finished the record his father started, Moroni explained what they used for the small, neatly carved characters of the Nephite record:

> We have written this record according to our knowledge, in the **characters** which are **called** among us the **reformed Egyptian**, being handed down and **altered by us according to our manner of speech**. And if our plates had been sufficiently large, we should have written in the Hebrew; but the Hebrew hath been **altered by us also**.
> (Mormon 4:11 [9:32], emphasis added)

The Nephites used only Egyptian "characters" for their writing and, apparently, not Egyptian language (at least not in the same way as would an Egyptian). This is at best an ambiguous point. How are we to understand it? Egyptian characters are not alphabet equivalent. A single character can mean many words, and their written form compresses language. We do not have anything equivalent to this in

---

[52] The dating for Abraham's life has been debated continually. For one discussion of the issue, see Hugh Nibley, *Abraham in Egypt*, Deseret Book (2000), pp. 114-118.
[53] See Mosiah 1:1 [1:4].

our common experience to make a meaningful analogy. Perhaps Pitman Shorthand would give an idea of it.

One other idea that may help a little is to think of Romance languages. All Romance languages use a common set of written characters but employ them for entirely different languages; the "reformed Egyptian" used "characters" to write a different quasi Hebrew-based language.

For a comparison: Spanish, French, Italian, Portuguese, and Romanian are all different languages that descended from Latin. They all use the Latin alphabet. But the words they write and the meanings of those words are different from one another. Occasionally, the different languages use identical letters for different words. In English (a non-Romance language), "mesa" means "an isolated, flat-topped hill with steep slopes." But in Spanish it means "table."

The English language descended from German. So did Icelandic, Norwegian, Danish, Swedish, and Scots. These languages also use the Latin alphabet, shared with the Latin-descended Romance languages. But try to imagine another language that employs pictographic and short-hand figures to convey both words and sentences. If you are moving information from such a language into any of the Latin alphabet languages, the result would be a far larger volume of translated text from the original text.

The Book of Mormon used Egyptian "characters" to write a non-Egyptian form of language to compress the material. How the Nephites achieved this over a millennium of "reforming" their written language was not clarified. However, if the actual plates of the Book of Mormon were to be examined by a modern Egyptian scholar, they would not be able to make any sense of it.

Hebrew is written and read from right to left. English is written from left to right. When I began learning the Hebrew alphabet, to help me remember the sounds, I would write my name using Hebrew characters in a left-to-right English format. "Dalet-Vav-Resh" was close enough, since vowels did not exist in Old Testament Hebrew. Since Hebrew would read these letters in reverse order, it would be read "Vav-Dalet" and pronounced something like "Ervid" and would mean "rod." And that's not my name.

Then when I began learning the Greek alphabet, to help me remember the sounds, I would also write my name using Greek characters. But I added the letter "v" because it was the only way I could think of to make it work: "Delta-Epsilon-Nu-V-Epsilon-Rho." Because "v" is English, it would not be used by a Greek speaker to figure the word out and, therefore, would be pronounced something like "Dener" and would mean "steward." That's also not my name.

When you use only characters borrowed from another language's alphabet but write things for your own native language, the result is a hybrid that requires an explanation—hence, Moroni's explanation that the Nephites only employed the Egyptian "characters" (and not the Egyptian language) in etching their record.[54] This idea will figure in later in this book.

Also significant is the assignment given to Joseph Smith to reform the Bible text. Joseph Smith began working on a revised Bible in June 1830. Joseph used the King James Version as his source text to accomplish this revision. There were few (if any) Greek or Hebrew materials used. Nothing was rendered from one language into another. The work was based on revelation, inspiration, and insight given to Joseph Smith by the Lord. The LDS Historian's Office has correctly called the work a "revision" of the Bible.[55] However technically inappropriate we may think it is to use the word "translation" for Joseph's work, it is always called a "translation" by the Lord in numerous revelations to Joseph.[56]

---

[54] Egyptian hieroglyphs are written in columns or at times from both left-to-right or right-to-left, and therefore, if only the alphabet was used and Hebrew format was kept, the Book of Mormon "Egyptian text" may well have seemed nonsensical to an Egyptologist. Hieratic was written from right-to-left.

[55] See *JSP, Revelations and Translations, Volume 4: Book of Abraham and Related Manuscripts*: "the Bible revision" (p. xv) and "When revising the Bible, Smith worked with a copy of the King James Version, apparently with no other instrument at hand" (p. xxiii).

[56] "It is not expedient in me that you should translate any more until you shall go to the Ohio" (T&C 20:1 [D&C 31:1]). "It shall not be given unto you to know any further than this until the New Testament be translated, and in it all these things shall be made known. Wherefore, I give unto you that you may now translate it" (T&C 31:13 [D&C 45:60-61]). "It is expedient to translate again, and inasmuch as it is practicable, to preach in the regions round about until conference. And after that, it is expedient to continue the work of translation until it be finished" (T&C 66:2 [D&C 73:3-4]). "For as we sat doing the work of translation which the Lord had appointed unto us..." (T&C 69:3 [D&C 76:15]). See also T&C 76:2; 88:1; 90:4 [D&C 90:12-18]; 91:1 [91]; 93:17 [92:52-53]; 97:3 [94:10-12]; 105:14; Lectures on Faith 2:5; and T&C 141:31 [D&C 124:88-90], all of which consistently refer to the process involved in revising the Bible as a "translation."

By November, the material about Adam, Cain, Abel, and the first murderer had been finished. The work advanced to include the Enoch material in December, and on 7 December 1830, Sidney Rigdon was commanded to act as scribe to "write for him." The project included correcting the Bible, as well as numerous additions. It was undertaken so that the Bible would be rewritten and, according to the Lord, to become *even as they are in [God's] own bosom* (T&C 18:6 [D&C 35:20]). The work of restoring Genesis advanced quickly. By February 1831, Genesis 1:1 through 5:12 was finished. These are eight chapters of the Book of Moses (as published in the Pearl of Great Price by the LDS Church). In these early materials, there are notable additions made regarding:

- Moses,[57]
- The Creation of this world,[58]
- An explanation of Satan's pre-Earth existence and history,[59]
- The fall of man,[60]
- Adam and Eve,[61] and
- Enoch[62] (among many others).

So much material involving Enoch was added in chapter 4 of Genesis that it has become referred to as the "Book of Enoch."

When the Genesis account got to Melchizedek, a flood of new material was provided.[63] In the new Melchizedek materials, we received clarifying information about the Holy Order:

> *Now Melchizedek was a man of faith who wrought righteousness. And when a child, he feared God, and stopped the mouths of lions, and quenched the violence of fire. And thus, having been approved of God, he was ordained a high priest after the Order of the covenant which God made with Enoch, it being after the Order of the Son of God, which Order came not by man, nor the will of men, neither by father nor mother, neither by beginning of days nor end of years,* **but of God.**

---

[57] See Genesis 1:1 to 2:2 [Moses 1:1-2:2].
[58] The Creation account in the new Genesis materials is provided as a revelation by God to Moses, beginning at Genesis 2:3 and going through 2:14 [Moses 2:3-3:25].
[59] See Genesis 2:15 [Moses 4:1-4].
[60] See Genesis 2:16-19 [Moses 4:5-31].
[61] See Genesis 3:1-4 [Moses 5:1-12].
[62] See Genesis 4:1-23 [Moses 6:26-7:69].
[63] See Genesis 7:12-21 [JST 14:25-40].

And it was delivered unto men by the calling of his own voice, according to his own will, unto as many as believed on his name.

For God, having sworn unto Enoch and unto his seed with an oath by himself that everyone being ordained after this Order and calling should have power, by faith, to break mountains, to divide the seas, to dry up waters, to turn them out of their course, to put at defiance the armies of nations, to divide the earth, to break every band, to stand in the presence of God, to do all things according to his will, according to his command subdue principalities and powers; and this by the will of the Son of God which was from before the foundation of the world. (Genesis 7:18-19 [JST 14:26-32], emphasis added)[64]

From this addition, we learn that faith—not priesthood—is the power that stops the mouths of lions and quenches the violence of fire. Also, ordination to the Holy Order comes from the voice of God and is conferred according to God's will. That will of God is predicated on two things:

- Belief on the name of God in **this** world, **and**
- The will of the Son of God **before the foundation** of this world.[65]

Despite the many additions and corrections to the Genesis text, very little was added in the Joseph Smith Bible revisions about Abraham. Given the importance of Abraham as a pivotal covenant Father, not adding an expanded account of his life to Genesis is a significant omission. The Lord told Abraham: *For as many as receive this gospel shall be called after your name and shall be accounted your seed, and shall rise up*

---

[64] These mighty works are all dependent upon "the will of the Son of God," as also mentioned when Nephi, son of Helaman, obtained power to control the elements. Nephi was a man who, according to God, "shalt not ask that which is contrary to [God's] will" (Helaman 3:19 [10:5]). Individuals are entrusted by God because God has faith in the man's determination to serve Him at all costs. Lecture 7 of Lectures on Faith deals with the effects of faith upon the whole of Creation. It includes, "When men begin to live by faith they begin to draw near to God. And when faith is perfected, they are like him; and because he is saved, they are saved also, for they will be in the same situation he is in because they have come to him; and when he appears, they shall be like him, for they will see him as he is" (Lectures on Faith 7:8).

[65] This coincides with Alma's later teaching, which was likely based on these same passages from the Moses materials included on the Brass Plates: "...being called and prepared from the foundation of the world, according to the foreknowledge of God, on account of their exceeding faith and good works in the first place, being left to choose good or evil; therefore they, having chosen good, and exercising exceeding great faith, are called with a holy calling" (Alma 9:10 [3:3]). They are sent into the world with authority "from the foundation of the world" to advance the salvation of others by their example in following the Savior.

and bless you, as unto their Father (Abraham 3:1 [2:10]). Given Abraham's importance, we should expect that any revision of Genesis would add as much about him as Genesis added about Adam and Enoch and Melchizedek. But the JST Bible did not do so.

If the Book of Abraham materials were added to the Genesis text, it would replace and expand the text from Genesis chapter 6 (midway in verse 8) through chapter 7 (midway through verse 4). The Book of Abraham supplies the missing important details we need to know that were omitted from the Genesis account of the Inspired Version of the Bible.

It appears that the foreknowledge of God made it unnecessary for a JST expansion of Genesis materials about Abraham. When Michael Chandler later sold four mummies, two papyrus scrolls, and some papyrus fragments (in July 1835) to buyers in Kirtland, Ohio, events were set in motion that resulted in adding Abrahamic details to our Scriptures. Three parties (one of whom was Joseph Smith) paid the $2,400 sale price.[66] The Book of Abraham was then produced after Joseph Smith got access to the papyri. Instead of being part of the JST Bible, it is called a "translation" of a papyrus scroll.

The "translation" began in Kirtland from July to November 1835 and produced the text from Abraham 1:1 through the first half of 4:2 in the Restoration Edition of Scripture.[67] There are three different copies of the translation made in Kirtland still in existence. These have been identified as Book of Abraham Manuscript A, B, and C.

- Manuscript A is in the handwriting of Frederick G. Williams.[68]
- Manuscript B is in the handwriting of Warren Parrish.[69]
- Manuscript C is in the handwriting of Warren Parrish and William W. Phelps.[70]

None of the Kirtland era translations of the Book of Abraham include the introduction to the book. That introduction attributes

---

[66] Joseph Coe, S. Andrews, and Joseph Smith & Co. each paid $800 for the purchase (see *JSP, Revelations and Translations, Volume 4: Book of Abraham and Related Manuscripts*, p. xx).
[67] In LDS Scripture, it is Abraham 1:1 through 2:18.
[68] See *JSP, Revelations and Translations, Volume 4: Book of Abraham and Related Manuscripts*, p. 192.
[69] Ibid., p. 203.
[70] Ibid., p. 217.

the text to a papyrus written: "by the hand of Abraham." That statement has been the focus of a great deal of controversy. It states: "A translation of some ancient records that have fallen into our hands, from the catacombs of Egypt, purporting to be the writings of Abraham while he was in Egypt, called 'The Book of Abraham, written by his own hand upon papyrus.'" Those words are in the handwriting of Willard Richards, and there is no existing source to explain why he added them to the publication of the Book of Abraham in the *Times & Seasons* in March 1842.[71]

A small library of material has been written on the relationship (or lack of relationship) between the remaining Joseph Smith Egyptian papyri fragments and the Book of Abraham. It is an understatement to say that subject is controversial. But given the importance of Abraham's status as the "Father of the righteous," it is important to discuss the controversy.

If one is objective, the text of the Book of Abraham presents insurmountable problems if it must satisfy the current scholarly understanding of the Egyptian papyri purchased from Michael Chandler.[72] If the authenticity of the Book of Abraham must be based on that, it is very problematic. That is not to say that the scholar's approach to this controversy is without its weaknesses.

The Egyptian language had two earliest forms; the first to develop was hieroglyphic and dates from before 4000 BC.[73] At about 390 AD, Byzantine Emperor Theodosius I closed all religious temples that he regarded as pagan throughout his empire. Because of this, hieroglyphs were no longer used. Egypt was inside his empire. Therefore, the Egyptian temples closed, and the hieroglyphic language was neglected and ultimately abandoned altogether. For 1500 years, the language was lost. Egyptian monuments remained, but no one had a clue what the hieroglyphics meant.

---

[71] Ibid., p. 245.
[72] The remnants of the preserved papyri date from the Ptolemaic era and are no older than 300 BC (and may have been only as old as 100 BC). The remaining fragments are part of the *Book of Breathings*, which themselves were composed long after the time of Abraham.
[73] Although Egyptian hieroglyphs are believed to date back to 4000 BC, the oldest remaining written texts are called the Pyramid Texts and date back to the 5th and 6th Dynasties (2613-2181 BC).

After being lost for a millennium-and-a-half, hieroglyphic interpretation has been recovered only in a small part through work based upon the Rosetta Stone. In July 1799, French soldiers were rebuilding a fort near the town of Rosetta and discovered a stone inscribed with three scripts: hieroglyphs in the top register, Greek at the bottom, and a script later identified as "Demotic" in the middle. Demotic was a still later form of Egyptian writing and was the common form spoken at the time the Rosetta Stone was originally carved.

Using the Greek from the Rosetta Stone as a guide to decipher the hieroglyphs, an attempt has been made to understand hieroglyphic Egyptian. The Rosetta stone contains a decree from Ptolemy V and dates from 196 BC. This is at the very end of a dying Egyptian culture, religion, language, and history. This era is known as the Ptolemaic dynasty.

Greeks controlled Egypt after Alexander the Great's conquest in 332 BC. When Alexander the Great died, his empire was divided between four generals.[74] At that time, General Ptolemy assumed control over Egypt.[75] The likelihood that the form of Egyptian hieroglyphic language dating from 196 BC is an accurate guide for understanding the way the language was understood millennia earlier is at best doubtful. If we accept the dating of 2100 BC for Abraham's life, there would have been two millennia of time separating the language of Abraham from the language of the Rosetta Stone.

> The most basic linguistic problem is to understand how language changes with time.
>
> Imagine you had a time machine. If you are like me, there would be many times and places that you would like to visit. In most of them, however, no one spoke English. If you could

---

[74] The four generals and their respective divisions were:
- A kingdom divided to General Cassander (circa 358–297 BC), consisting of Macedonia, most of Greece, and parts of Thrace.
- To General Lysimachus (circa 361–281 BC) was divided Lydia, Ionia, Phrygia, and other parts of present-day Turkey.
- To General Seleucus (died 281 BC) was divided present-day Iran, Iraq, Syria, and parts of Central Asia (later known as the Seleucid Empire).
- To General Ptolemy I (died 283 BC) was divided Egypt and neighboring regions.

[75] Ptolemy's descendants ruled Egypt for 275 years in what is named the Ptolemaic Dynasty (305-330 BC), ending with Cleopatra who lived during the lives of Julius Caesar, Mark Anthony, and Octavius (Caesar Augustus).

not afford the Six-Month-Immersion Trip to, say, ancient Egypt, you would have to limit yourself to a time and place where you could speak the language. Consider, perhaps, a trip to England. How far back in time could you go and still be understood? Say we go to London in the year 1400 CE.

As you emerge from the time machine, a good first line to speak, something reassuring and recognizable, might be the opening line of the Lord's Prayer. The first line in a conservative, old-fashioned version of the Modern Standard English would be, "*Our Father, who is in heaven, blessed be your name.*" In the English of 1400, as spoken by Chaucer, you would say, "*Oure fadir that art in heunes, halwid be thy name.*" Now turn the dial back another four hundred years to 1000 CE, and in Old English, or Anglo-Saxon, you would say, "*Faeader, ure thu the eart on heofonum, si thin nama gehalgod.*" A chat with Alfred the Great would be out of the question.

Most normal spoken languages over the course of a thousand years undergo enough change that speakers at either end of the millennium, attempting a conversation, would have difficulty understanding each other.[76]

Consequently, it would be surprising–bordering on miraculous–if the way Egyptian hieroglyphs were understood at the time of the Rosetta Stone proves identical to the way they were understood two-thousand years earlier in the lifetime of Abraham.[77]

That having been said, Egyptologists believe they have fragments of the Joseph Smith papyri translated by him to comprise the Book of Abraham. They rely on their ability to interpret these fragments using reconstructed Ptolemaic Egyptian. Using their skill-set, they are confident that the fragments do not contain a Book of Abraham but are, instead, an Egyptian *Book of Breathings* (sen-sen papyri). They

---

[76] David W. Anthony, *The Horse, The Wheel And Language: How Bronze-Age Riders from the Eurasian Steppes Shaped the Modern World*, (Princeton University Press, 2007), p. 22, footnotes omitted, italics in original.

[77] "...the ancient scribes who produced these documents were often unable to read what they were writing. By the Twenty-first Dynasty, Naville noted, the 'ignorance of the scribes' reached the point (toward which it had long been steadily trending) of complete miscomprehension of their own texts, betrayed by the 'common habit of copying entire sections backwards'" (Nibley, *An Approach to the Book of Abraham*, p. 99).

conclude Joseph Smith was unable to "translate" the source document.

There are multiple ways apologists have dealt with this problem:

- One approach, including Hugh Nibley's analysis, is that there was an Egyptian papyri source but dispute that the papyrus fragments we have are the actual text Joseph translated.[78] This group of apologists assume what Joseph actually translated was destroyed in the great Chicago fire. The approach accepts Willard Richards' *Times & Seasons* introduction explaining it is a translation of records from the catacombs of Egypt, originating with Abraham.

- A second apologetic approach is to claim there never was a source papyrus for the Book of Abraham. This position ignores Willard Richards' *Times & Seasons* introduction. This approach claims the source for the Book of Abraham was entirely revelation from Heaven. The LDS Church now seems to accept this view.[79]

- A third apologetic approach is that the Michael Chandler papyri were indeed the source for the Book of Abraham, and the text can actually be recovered using the Joseph Smith Papyri.[80] These advocates make a full-throated defense of Willard Richards' *Times & Seasons* introduction. Until the scholarly understanding of Egyptology challenged Mormons, this was the overwhelming position of those who accept the

---

[78] See *The Message of the Joseph Smith Papyri: An Egyptian Endowment*, First Edition 1975, pp. 1-3: "...the Prophet Joseph himself has supplied us with the most conclusive evidence that the manuscript today identified as the Book of Breathings, J.S. Papyri X and XI was not in his opinion the source of the Book of Abraham" (p. 2, emphasis in original).

[79] After quoting from the *Wilford Woodruff Journal* that attributed the translation to "the Urim & Thummim," the LDS Historian's Office uses Orson Pratt's reminiscence that implied Joseph Smith's method was similar to other revelations. It is called "inspiration without the use of a seer stone." The Historian's Office then concludes: "It is unclear when in 1835 Joseph Smith began creating the existing Book of Abraham manuscripts or what relationship the Book of Abraham manuscripts have to the Egyptian-language documents" (*JSP, Revelations and Translations, Volume 4: Book of Abraham and Related Manuscripts*, pp. xxiv-xxv).

[80] See, e.g., Goble, Edwin, *Joseph Smith's Egyptian, the Book of Abraham, and the Ancient World*, CreateSpace Independent Publishing Platform; 2nd edition (January 4, 2016), and his recent essay, *As Practiced by the Ancients: The Grammar and Alphabet of the Egyptian Language as 19th Century Metadata Or, a Pictographic Book of Abraham for Grammatomancy*, which theorizes the Book of Abraham was divined/revealed after being inspired by metadata deliberately embedded in the Hor Sensen Papyrus.

Book of Abraham as Scripture. In this arena of argument, there is a belief that the hieroglyphs contained hidden, esoteric meaning encoded in their form. As Dan Vogel describes it, "...other, more spiritual, mystical, and theologically powerful messages were encoded in their pictographic etymologies."[81] Vogel rejects this idea.

There are other approaches. All of them address the issue of what perspective should be used to explain Joseph's translation.

- Should we assume the illustrations were original to Abraham? If so, then to interpret them, maybe we should look to how Egyptians in Abraham's day–or Abraham himself–would have understood them.

- Or should we assume the illustrations were original to Abraham but were modified over time for other uses by the ancient Egyptians?

- Or do we assume the illustrations were connected to the Book of Abraham when the Joseph Smith papyri were created in the Ptolemaic period?

- Do we need to consider what Egyptians of that time thought these drawings represented?

- Or should we assume the illustrations were connected to the Book of Abraham for the first time in the Ptolemaic period, but to interpret them we ought to look at what Egyptian priests (integrating Jewish, Greek, and Mesopotamian religious practices into native Egyptian practices) would have thought about them?

- Or should we instead look at how Jews of that era would have understood them?

---

[81] *Book of Abraham Apologetics: A Review and Critique*, (Signature Books, 2021), p. 67, quoting from R. John Williams, cited as, "The Ghost and the Machine: Plates and Paratext in The Book of Mormon," in *Americanist Approaches to the Book of Mormon*, Elizabeth Fenton and Jared Hickman eds. (New York: Oxford University Press, 2019), 79n45.

- Or were the illustrations never part of an ancient Book of Abraham but instead adapted by Joseph Smith to depict the ancient text he revealed/translated?[82]

In the give-and-take following deciphering the Rosetta Stone and the research done to develop some understanding of the Egyptian language, the apologists who think the Book of Abraham was directly translated from the Joseph Smith papyri appear to hold the weaker position.[83] However, that is not the end of the matter.

> In every case in which he has produced a translation, Joseph Smith has made it clear that his inspiration is by no means bound to any ancient text but is free to take wings at any time. To insist, as the critics do, that "translation" may be understood only in the sense in which they choose to understand it, while the Prophet clearly demonstrates that he intends it to be taken in a very different sense, is to make up the rules of the game one is playing as well as being the umpire.[84]

Since Joseph Smith did not explain how the text was "translated," that issue is left to conjecture.[85] The entire debate between Egyptian scholars and apologists centers on the translation process. However, Joseph Smith did not use the term "translation" as would a scholar.[86] One example illustrates the difference:

While Oliver Cowdery was the scribe during the Book of Mormon translation, he and Joseph discussed whether the Apostle John died

---

[82] These different approaches are suggested by Pearl of Great Price Central in a 6 January 2020 article: *Approaching the Facsimiles: Book of Abraham Insight #27*, pearlofgreatpricecentral.org/approaching-the-facsimiles/

[83] See Ritner, Robert K. *The Joseph Smith Egyptian Papyri: A Complete Edition*, Smith-Pettit Foundation (2011) for a recap by an Egyptian scholar who is critical of Hugh Nibley, Michael Rhodes, and John Gee.

[84] Nibley, *An Approach to the Book of Abraham*, p. 4.

[85] "No known first-person account from Joseph Smith exists to explain the translation of the Book of Abraham, and the scribes who worked on the project and others who claimed knowledge of the process provided only vague or general reminiscences" (JSP, Revelations and Translations, Volume 4: Book of Abraham and Related Manuscripts, p. xxiii).

[86] "We can save ourselves much rumination if we accept at the outset that Joseph Smith never did document-to-document translation based on a knowledge of two languages, except as an exercise in his Hebrew class in the winter of 1835-36" (Karl C. Sandberg, *Knowing Brother Joseph Again: The Book of Abraham and Joseph Smith as Translator*, Dialogue: A Journal of Mormon Thought, Vol. 22, No. 4 [Winter 1989] p. 19).

or continued on Earth. The question was answered by a revelation. The written account in our Scriptures about the answer includes this explanation: *A revelation given to Joseph Smith Jr. and Oliver Cowdery in Harmony, Pennsylvania, April 1829, when they desired to know whether John, the beloved disciple, tarried on earth. Translated from parchment, written and hid up by himself* (JSH 13:17).[87] Joseph did not have the parchment. Therefore, there was no parchment source for the revelation. It came by Joseph Smith receiving it from God through *the Urim and Thummim* (ibid.).

Sidney Rigdon arrived in Fayette during December 1830, as the Bible revision was already underway. The project involved editing and correcting the Bible. That project was also consistently referred to as a "translation" of the Bible,[88] even though it would more correctly be called an "inspired revision." On December 7, 1830, the commandment was given to Sidney Rigdon: *You shall write for him, and the scriptures shall be given, even as they are in my own bosom, to the salvation of my own elect...* (T&C 18:6 [D&C 35:20]). This helps explain what the term "translated" meant for the Bible revision project. It clearly refers to something different than how the term is generally used and understood.

When Enoch's City was taken to Heaven, it is described as being "translated"[89] or a "translation." For Enoch, "translated" meant moving someone from Earth into Heaven and changing him or her so they could survive there.[90] This meaning can also be understood and used for the "translation" of the parchment of John. It means taking something recorded and preserved in Heaven[91] and moving it back to the Earth where it had been lost.

I think that the word "translated" as it refers to the Book of Abraham should be understood in this sense: It was something recorded in Heaven, and it was moved back to the Earth where it had

---

[87] Italics in original.
[88] See, e.g., T&C 20:1 [D&C 37:1-2]; 31:13 [45:60-63]; 66:2 [73:3-6]; 69:3 [76:11-17]; 88:1; 90:4 [90:12-18]; 91:1 [91]; 93:17 [93:52-53]; 97:3 [94:10-12]; Lectures on Faith 2:5; and T&C 141:32 [D&C 124:91-96].
[89] See Hebrews 1:38 [11:5-6]; Ether 6:20 [15:33-34]; Lectures on Faith 2:41,107,113; T&C 140:13; 154:15 [D&C 107:48-49].
[90] The word is also used to describe the three Nephite disciples whose bodies were similarly altered, but they were to remain on Earth. Here, however, they were not to suffer death or bodily pain nor be tempted by Satan (see 3 Nephi 13:6 [28:36-40]).
[91] See, e.g., Deuteronomy 9:13 [31:24-29]; T&C 141:32 [D&C 124:91-96]; 150:7 [127:11-12]; 151:5-7 [128:7-9].

been lost. Regardless of whether or not conveying Abraham's testimony from Heaven back to the Earth required a surviving papyrus scroll, that question is not as important as the accuracy and truthfulness of the Book of Abraham account that originated with Father Abraham. Only if the text is true, accurate, and legitimately Abraham's would it be worthy for canonizing as Scripture. **Joseph Smith clearly intended for the Book of Abraham to be Scripture.**[92]

Apart from using the word "translation," the content of the material bears all the indicia of an ancient record from the time of Father Abraham.[93] The account in the Book of Abraham can be compared with Abraham's history in Genesis. The comparison shows there are over a dozen details added through the Book of Abraham account that are missing from Genesis. For example:

- The famine in the homeland of Ur,
- Haran's (Abraham's brother) death in the famine,
- Terah (Abraham's father) repented of his idolatry,
- Terah returned to idolatry,
- Believers became the "seed of Abraham" and inherited the blessings through him,
- Abraham held priesthood,

---

[92] Joseph wrote an announcement for the *Times & Seasons* on March 1, 1842 explaining what he intended for the Book of Abraham: "In future. I design to furnish much original matter, which will be found of enestimable advantage to the saints,– & to all who– desire a knowledge of the kingdom of God.– and as it is not practicable to bring for the the new translation. of the Scriptures. & varioes records of ancint date. & great worth to this gen[e]ration in book <the usual> form. by books. I shall prenit [print] specimens of the same in the Times & Seasons as fast. as time & space will admit. so that the honest in heart may be cheerd & comforted and go on their way rejoi[ci]ng.– as their souls become exp[an]ded.– & their undestandig [understanding] enlightend, by a knowledg of what Gods work through the fathers. in former days, as well as what He is about to do in Latter Days – To fulfil the words of the fathers.– In the penst [present] no. will be found the Commencmet of the Records discoverd in Egypt. some time since. as penend by the hand. of Father Abraham. which I shall contin[u]e to translate & publish as fast as possible till the whole is completed" (*JSP, Documents, Volume 9,* p. 206-7). This announcement was never printed in the *Times & Seasons*; however, publication of the Book of Abraham began in that edition (Vol. III, no. 9).

[93] The word "translation" has been used as the basis for criticism of the Book of Abraham. Ritner, for example, argues, "In the Book of Abraham Smith's explicit references to texts in the Facsimiles and his use of the subtitle 'Translated from the Papyrus, by Joseph Smith,' can mean only that he misrepresented or did not understand the concept of translation" (Ritner, *The Joseph Smith Egyptian Papyri,* supra, p. 137, ftnote. 331). He later adds, "Nibley can only defend Smith's use of the term 'translation' by undercutting the very meaning of the term" (ibid. p. 142, ftnote. 358). These are meaningless jabs, because the word was clearly NOT used by Joseph Smith to hold the traditional meaning.

- Abraham earnestly sought God,
- An angel of the Lord was sent to rescue Abraham,
- Abraham was familiar with Egyptian gods,
- Abraham was 62 years old (not 75, as in Genesis) when he left Haran,[94]
- Abraham made converts while in Haran,
- Abraham prayed for God to end the famine in Chaldea, and
- The Lord instructed Abram to say that Sarai was his sister.[95]

All of these differences (related to Abraham) can be found in ancient sources recorded in non-Biblical [texts].[96] If ancient sources confirm events set out in the Book of Abraham **did happen** in Abraham's life, it is hard to simply dismiss the validity of the book as inauthentic.[97] It only makes the most sense to consider the text itself when deciding the validity of the Book of Abraham.

> One might dismiss a single element found in a nonbiblical tradition that parallels the Book of Abraham as mere coincidence. However, when a large number of such elements come together from diverse times and places, they overwhelmingly support the Book of Abraham as an ancient text. There are far too many references to Terah as an idolator, Abraham as a sacrificial victim, Abraham as an astronomer, and Abraham as a missionary to lightly dismiss their antiquity. In addition, many other distinctive elements found in these traditions, though not repeated frequently,

---

[94] In Genesis, it is Terah who leaves Ur and takes Abram with him: "And Terah took Abram (his son), and Lot (the son of Haran—his son's son) and Sarai (his daughter-in-law—his son Abram's wife), and went forth with them from Ur of the Chaldees to go into the land of Canaan" (Genesis 6:8 [11:31]). In the Book of Abraham, the Lord commands Abram to depart, "and also my father followed after me" (Abraham 2:5 [2:4]).

[95] See *Traditions About the Early Life of Abraham*, (FARMS 2001), p. xxii.

[96] "Taken as a whole, the Abraham traditions contained in this book show that all of the elements in this list are attested to in nonbiblical traditions to one degree or another. Some elements attested only in Abraham 2 [LDS] but not in Genesis 11 and 12 [KJV] appear regularly in nonbiblical texts. For instance, the themes of Terah's idolatry, an angel rescuing Abraham, and Abraham making converts in Haran are so well attested by a large cross section of traditions that it appears odd the biblical account does not include them. Abraham 1 and 3 [LDS] are not attested at all in the Bible, yet they also contain elements that are well evidenced in nonbiblical traditions. Abraham 1 contains the sacrifice of Abraham, Abraham as a record keeper, and the destruction of idols, and Abraham 3 [LDS] contains an account of Abraham's knowledge and use of astronomy" (Ibid., pp. xxii-xxiii).

[97] For a brief recap of numerous details from the Book of Abraham that are consistent with other ancient sources unknown in Joseph Smith's day, see Nibley, *Abraham in Egypt*, supra, pp. 648-654.

add to the overall strength of the unique elements found in the Book of Abraham.[98]

Facsimile 3 includes the comment that the scene depicts *Abraham...reasoning upon the principles of astronomy in the king's court*. This echoes the account by Josephus that (to the Egyptians) Abraham, "...confuted the reasonings they made use of, every one for their own practices, demonstrating that such reasonings were vain and void of truth; whereupon he was admired by them in those conferences as a very wise man, and one of great sagacity, when he discoursed on any subject." Josephus explained that Abraham, "...communicated to them arithmetic, and delivered to them the science of astronomy."[99]

The oldest written Egyptian material is the *Pyramid Texts* that date from the 5th and 6th Dynasties.[100] At the time of those writings, the original Pharaonic imitative religion was already approximately 1,000 years old. There is no way to know how well the religion was preserved between the first Pharaoh's initial imitation and a millennium later when the *Pyramid Texts* were written.

Egypt had a complicated theological development that morphed over time. The Horus stellar religion is very early. The Osirian religion (sometimes linked to lunar theology) does not arise until nearly 1,000 years after the *Pyramid Texts* at Saqqara and, arguably, most reflects the religion of the New Kingdom. That theology differs from the beliefs of the Old Kingdom religion. It was the Old Kingdom theology that is closer to that of Adam. Finally, the Memphite religion of Ra apparently begins in the late Old Kingdom. However, Ra (as the sun god) is syncretized to Ahmon (the god of light). The figure of Ahmon is present in both the star cult and the sun cult. As Egyptian religion changed at the time of the New Kingdom, nothing remained of the star cult.

---

[98] Ibid., p. xxxv. See also *Traditions About the Early Life of Abraham*, supra, Index A, pp. 537-547 where is listed material absent from the Genesis account and other parts of the Bible but which are in the Book of Abraham and other non-biblical ancient sources. The materials are listed by topic and subtopic with citations to the various sources.

[99] Josephus, *The Antiquity of the Jews*, Book 1, Chapter 2, ¶2.

[100] They were inscribed in the 5th and 6th Dynasties, but the texts reckon from earlier materials dating perhaps 1,000 or more years earlier. Evidence of worship of Ahman goes back to pre-dynastic Egypt.

The Book of Abraham's exposition on the sun, earth, planets, and stars fits neatly into the cosmological issues perplexing the rulers of 9th Dynasty Egypt. And by the way, the Joseph Smith rendering of the word "planets" is criticized by a number of scholars as being not a term that was understood at the time. But the word "planets" means "a star that wanders." The ancients referred to fixed stars, and also to stars that wandered. "Planets" simply is referring to the stars that move in the sky overhead. And so, calling them "planets" is not at all problematic.

There are many connections between the language of Egypt and the Restoration. The hieroglyphic form of Egyptian was used primarily to record religious texts and was the more formal or sacred form of their writing. A second, less formal form developed early in Egyptian language evolution and is called "hieratic." This second form was cursive and was the more likely form used on the Brass Plates. It is arrogant to assume that Ptolemaic era writing is a sound basis for ciphering backward over 2,000 years to decode Egyptian Hieroglyphics. In the end, the question must be asked: Do you trust a scholar's attempt to reconstruct antiquity using a partial record from 196 BC when it conflicts with the revelation given to Joseph Smith who claimed to be a prophet, seer, and translator? Or do you believe God could inspire a prophet to recover a lost record from an ancient patriarch? It is one or the other.

It is significant that Joseph Smith claimed that the Old Testament written on the Brass Plates, as well as the record of the Nephites,[101] were written in Egyptian. At the time and under the circumstances, Joseph Smith had little reason to make such a claim. With what we now know, it would be an error to claim otherwise. The choice is between Joseph being prescient or prophetic.

Joseph revealed that Adam and his immediate posterity wrote the first records of God's dealing with mankind. It was called *a book of remembrance* (Genesis 3:14 [Moses 6:5-6]). That record was written in *a language which was pure and undefiled* (ibid.). We know those records existed during Abraham's life (thousands of years later): *The records of the Fathers, even the Patriarchs, ...the Lord, my God, preserved in my own hands* (Abraham 2:4 [1:31]).

---

[101] See Mormon 4:11 [9:31-37].

By the time of Moses, however, the original records were lost. Moses had to restore the record of the Creation based on the revelation he received directly from the Lord. Moses was commanded:

> *You shall write the things which I shall speak. And in a day when the children of men shall esteem my words as naught and take many of them from the book which you shall write, behold, I will raise up another like unto you, and they shall be had again among the children of men, among even as many as shall believe.* (Genesis 1:7 [Moses 1:40-41])

Pharaoh's daughter raised Moses from birth. She named him and treated him as "her son."[102] Accordingly, when Moses was commanded to write the record revealed to him by the Lord, he would have recorded it in the language he understood: the language his adopted mother taught him, which was Egyptian. This detail is exactly what the Book of Mormon explains about the Brass Plates. Moses replaced the lost records of the Fathers by revelation from God. That record is described in the Book of Mormon as *the records which were engraven upon the plates of brass* and were composed *in the language of the Egyptians* (Mosiah 1:1 [1:3-4]). Ask yourself the likelihood of a New England farm boy in 1829 choosing to claim the Old Testament was recorded in the Egyptian language? It is a remarkable bulls-eye detail, unlikely to have occurred to a youthful religious swindler. (But of course, Joseph was an actual prophet, and therefore, God revealed to him the truths he recounted.)

Since Joseph translated over 500 pages of what was likely derived from Hieratic Egyptian for the Book of Mormon, he read and understood one version of that language better than any scholar, including all who have lived since the discovery of the Rosetta Stone. Because I accept Joseph's claims of being a prophet, seer, and translator at face value, it is easy for me to resolve conflicts over Egyptian texts in favor of Joseph and against the scholarly critics.

Joseph Smith Papers, Volume 4 of the Revelations and Translations has copies of Egyptian Alphabet materials produced by Joseph's scribes: Oliver Cowdery,[103] William W. Phelps,[104] and Warren Parrish.[105] Teryl

---

[102] See Exodus 1:5 [2:5-10].
[103] Egyptian Alphabet A, pp. 56-72 and Egyptian Alphabet B, pp. 74-83.
[104] Egyptian Alphabet A, pp. 56-72, and Egyptian Alphabet C, pp. 86-93.
[105] Egyptian Alphabet C, pp. 86-93.

Givens has taken the position that these texts prove, "The Book of Abraham manuscripts, unlike their Book of Mormon counterpart, bear clear evidence of reworking, revising, and editing. This was no spontaneous channeling of a finished product by any stretch."[106] He interprets these as proof that Joseph Smith engaged in a very complex deciphering process to produce the Book of Abraham using the hieroglyphics from the *Book of Breathings*.

When I first saw the Egyptian Alphabet materials, it appeared to me to be an attempt to reverse engineer Joseph Smith's translation of the Book of Abraham by using the *Book of Breathing* papyrus. Recall that Oliver Cowdery had attempted to translate the Book of Mormon and failed in that attempt. When he failed, the Lord explained his failure to him, stating:

> Behold, you have not understood; you have supposed that I would give it unto you when you took no thought save it was to ask me. But behold, I say unto you that you must study it out in your mind, then you must ask me if it be right, and if it is right, I will cause that your bosom shall burn within you; therefore, you shall feel that it is right. (JSH 13:26 [D&C 9:7-8])

Two of the three Egyptian Alphabet studies (A and B) were in whole (or in major part) the study of Oliver Cowdery. It appears these were the result of Oliver's attempts to follow the Lord's guidance after his failure to successfully translate the Book of Mormon. When he failed in 1829, the Lord said there were *other records have I that I will give unto you power that you may assist to translate* (ibid., vs. 24 [9:2]). It seems apparent the Egyptian Alphabet study in late 1835 was Oliver's (and the other scribes') attempt to validate the translation process and act on the earlier promise to Oliver.

Teryl Givens' speculation that the Egyptian Alphabet is Joseph Smith's study of the papyrus is refuted by John S. Thompson in his article, "'We May Not Understand Our Words': The Book of Abraham and the Concept of Translation in The Pearl of Greatest Price."[107] Thompson shows from contemporary sources that Joseph's translation was accomplished quickly and before the Egyptian

---

[106] Terryl Givens with Brian M. Hauglid, *The Pearl of Greatest Price: Mormonism's Most Controversial Scripture* (New York: Oxford University Press, 2019), p. 201.
[107] *Interpreter: A Journal of Latter-day Saint Faith and Scholarship*, Volume 41, 2020, pp. 1-48.

Alphabet documents were created. It is clear from his examination of the historical record that the scribes did their deciphering work of the Egyptian characters **after** the translation of the Book of Abraham had been done.[108] Accordingly, using the Egyptian Alphabet materials to try to understand the translation process is not likely to help us understand what Joseph did (but much more likely to help us understand his scribes' attempt to understand Joseph's translating work).

It is not possible to resolve this question. Those directly involved **were never asked**, and they failed to leave a clear account of **what** the Egyptian Alphabet documents were, **why** they were produced, and **how** they relate to translation of the Book of Abraham. This has resulted in debate between scholar-critics and scholar-apologists.

The latest writer to weigh in on the subject, Dan Vogel, deals with the absence of hard answers by arguing the meaning and import of ambiguous details.[109] As a lawyer, I appreciate his argumentation. However, since I care about the subject and would like to know the truth, the arguments from implication in the absence of proof cannot be fully convincing. The souls of men must not be trifled with.[110]

In arguing from the absence of hard historical evidence, Vogel urges his belief that:

> ...what is required in any treatment of the Book of Abraham is not fluency in hieroglyphics or a belief in Joseph Smith's prophetic calling, but a firm, clear-headed understanding of the methods of history and of the relevant nineteenth-century historical sources. Anything else is counter-productive.[111]

He makes the argument that the Kirtland Egyptian Papers were not created after the translation but were used to create/translate the Book of Abraham. His arguments are somewhat persuasive.

---

[108] The Kirtland-era translation completed Abraham 1:1 through 2:18 apparently in the two months following the purchase from Chandler. The Egyptian Alphabet materials were composed in the months following.
[109] *Book of Abraham Apologetics: A Review and Critique*, supra.
[110] See T&C 138:18.
[111] *Book of Abraham Apologetics: A Review and Critique*, p. xvii.

However, his analysis is advocacy, and his writing betrays the assumptions necessary for his conclusions. The book necessarily reflects a scholar's caution in the absence of certainty. Although his work is interesting, well written, and attempts to make reasonable points, the information we have available does not let us really resolve anything about the Kirtland Egyptian Papers. Everything is arguable. Vogel's arguments certainly belong in the debate, but in the end, it is only argument (like so much else involving the Book of Abraham). A few examples of how he supports his arguments are:

- "implies a process of translation" (p. 1)
- "would have observed" (p. 9)
- "which implies a translation scenario" (p. 11)
- "This clearly implies" (p. 12)
- "Whether the characters were written before, after, or simultaneously with the English text is ultimately irrelevant" (p. 12)
- "It only makes sense" (p. 13)
- "implies that" (p. 14)
- "there would be no need to" (p. 14)
- "The strongest evidence" (p. 17)
- "more careful analysis shows" (p. 17)
- "the simplest way to explain" (p. 17)
- "This suggests" (p. 18)
- "most reasonably explained as" (p. 18)
- "was likely due to" (p. 18)
- "may have dictated" (p. 19)
- "no evidence to support" (p. 20)
- "no justification to theorize about a missing source" (p. 20)
- "mark the possible time" (p. 21)
- "This is likely the exact time" (p. 21)
- "evidence suggests" (p. 22)
- "which could suggest that" (p. 22)
- "there is strong evidence supporting" (p. 22)
- "is best explained as" (p. 25)
- "a much more likely explanation" (p. 25)
- "probably suggestion" (p. 25)
- "two possible instances" (p. 25)
- "he evidently began" (p. 25)
- "are best explained as" (p. 25)
- "a more likely explanation is that" (p. 25)
- "could easily lose his place" (p. 27)

- "does not provide definitive evidence" (p. 27)
- "implying that it is not complete" (p. 28)
- "indicating that" (p. 28)
- "a reconstruction of events that best explains" (p. 28)
- "was apparently unaware" (p. 30)
- "may have added to William's confusion" (p. 30)
- "the possibility that" (p. 30)
- "had evidently copied" (p. 31)
- "We may not know exactly" (p. 31)
- "the scenario I have proposed explains" (p. 31)
- "is supported by strong, compelling evidence" (p. 31)
- "should be seen as" (p. 31)
- "therefore likely came from" (p. 34)
- "may have" (p. 34)
- "would have appeared in" (p. 35)
- "no doubt with the help of" (p. 36)
- "it would be a mistake to assume" (p. 37)
- "seemed to ignore" (p. 37)
- "he seemingly ignored" (p. 37)
- "The details of Smith's participation in the creation of his own history are not…well known, but apparently" (p. 39)
- "were likely the result of" (p. 39)
- "Apparently, there was some hesitation" (p. 50)
- "is instructive, although piecing together what was intended is not always clear and necessitates some conjecture" (p. 54)
- "possibly from" (p. 55)
- "may have taken from" (p. 55)
- "is probably more than coincidence" (p. 56)
- "This is a problem from the theory" (p. 57)
- (and so on)

Whether I agree or disagree with his interpretation does not give me the actual historical certitude that would answer the most important questions about the Book of Abraham's creation (or "translation," as the term was used and understood by Joseph Smith). There are debaters on both sides. They all make arguments to support their desired conclusion. Familiarity with the Egyptian language (insofar as the Ptolemaic period Rosetta Stone material permits the language to be resurrected) causes the Egyptologists to be dogmatic. They speak in firm declaratives. But Joseph Smith saw God the Father, His Son, Michael, Raphael, Gabriel, Peter, James, and John, and a host of angels who declared their dispensations, keys, rights, honors, and glory.[112] Joseph also spoke in firm declaratives. They line up on opposite sides, and **we** must choose between them.

The best evidence of translation authenticity is the text itself. As Hugh Nibley put it, "...it is the Book of Abraham that is on trial, not Joseph Smith as an Egyptologist, nor the claims and counterclaims to scholarly recognition by squabbling publicity seekers."[113] The text of the Book of Abraham is compelling and adds important theological information I believe to be vital to understanding the religion I accept and Abraham's role in God's plan for this Creation. More importantly, I accept the idea that it adds information vital to salvation.

I believe it is also important that Joseph intended the Book of Abraham **as** Scripture. He wrote on March 1, 1842:

> In future. I design to furnish much original matter, which will be found of enestimable adventage to the saints,– &...all who– desire a knowledge of the kingdom of God.– and as it is not practicable to bring forthe the new translation. of...Scriptures. & varioes records of ancint date. & great worth to this gen[e]ration in...<the usual> form. by books. I shall prenit [print] specimens of the same in the Times & Seasons as fast. as time & space will admit. so that the honest in heart may be cheerd & comforted and go on their way rejoi[ci]ng.– as their souls become exp[an]ded.– & their undestandig [understanding] enlightend, by a knowledg of what Gods work through the fathers. in former days, as well as what He is about to do in Latter Days– To fulfil the words of the fathers.–
>
> In the penst [present] no. will be found the Commencmet of the Records discoverd in Egypt. some time since. as penend by the hand. of Father Abraham. which I shall contin[u]e to translate & publish as fast as possible till the whole is completed.[114]

That was composed by Joseph to accompany what was published in the *Times and Seasons* as the first installment of the Book of Abraham.

---

[112] See T&C 151:15 [D&C 128:19-21]; 157:31.
[113] *Abraham in Egypt*, (Deseret Book 2000), p. 3.
[114] *JSP, Documents, Volume 9*, p. 206-7.

If Joseph Smith regarded the Book of Abraham as Scripture, I do not want to dismiss it because an Egyptologist cannot read it in the remaining papyrus fragments some claim as the source for the book.

It is not at all clear that Egyptology is **even relevant** to an analysis of the Book of Abraham. The narrative text begins in a location named Ur of the Chaldeans. The book states 32 times it does not cover events **in Egypt**. There are 13 times the location is Ur. Another 16 times the events happened in Haran, Jershon, Sechem, Morah, or Canaan. Then before ending, it clarifies three times the account is not about events **in Egypt**. Here is a brief review of the many times it clarifies it is **NOT** an account from Egypt:

- Facsimile No. 1 illustrates an event that took place in Ur, not in Egypt.

- Abraham's record begins: *In the land of the Chaldeans* (Abraham 1:1 [1:1]).

- When Abraham was bound and put on the altar to be sacrificed –as illustrated in Facsimile No. 1– it was upon *the altar which was built in the land of the Chaldeans* (ibid., vs. 3 [1:8]).

- It was constructed *after the form of a bedstead, such as was had among the Chaldeans* (ibid., vs. 4 [1:13]). The record is silent about whether Egyptians had any similar altar. Scholarly critics explain the Egyptian funerary practice associated with the Chaldean altar with the customary lion-headed funerary bier on which embalming–not human sacrifice–is typically depicted by any similar Egyptian hieroglyphic. Again, however, that is not particularly helpful to understanding what happened in Ur of the Chaldeans. Nor does that criticism address Chaldean behavior, religious rites, or altar design.

- The Book of Abraham does not give us any Egyptian names but explains Chaldean (not Egyptian) terminology is used.

- The book explains that Facsimile No. 1 shows *the figures at the beginning, which manner of the figures is called by the Chaldeans Kahleenos, which signifies hieroglyphics* (ibid. [1:14]). This word is what the Chaldeans would call the vignette, not what an Egyptian would. The explanation is provided because the Chaldean word is different from the Egyptian term. On this point, an Egyptologist's criticism is of little help to authenticate or refute the Book of Abraham.

To the eye of an Egyptologist, the four figures under the lion couch in Facsimile No. 1 are canopic jars. They are the four receptacles used in Egyptian embalming practice for the liver, lungs, stomach, and intestines. The liver jar is, to the Egyptians, the human-headed Imseti.[115] The lung jar is to them the baboon-headed Hapi.[116] The stomach jar is the jackal-headed Duamutef.[117] The intestine jar is the falcon-headed Qebehsnuef.[118] None of those Egyptian names are used in the Book of Abraham by the Chaldeans.

But then again, the text is not about Egypt but about the local practice of those living in Ur of the Chaldeans. In that place, nothing Abraham understood about these four figures suggests they were jars. Instead, Abraham understood they were Chaldean idols before which human sacrifices were performed. The names of these idols in the land of the Chaldeans were Elkenah, Zibnah, Mahmackrah, and Koash. Abraham's account is not about the gods of Egypt. It is about the gods of the Chaldeans.

Egyptologists criticize the account that Abraham (as well as three virgins before him) was offered as a human sacrifice.[119] Many scholars dispute Egyptians offered human sacrifices.[120] To an Egyptologist, the mention of human sacrifice is evidence the Book of

---

[115] Egyptians associated the liver with emotion and, therefore, depicted Imseti as human-headed. It was also depicted wearing the nemes headcloth, a striped headband.

[116] Depicted as a blue or green baboon-headed human, regarded as the god responsible for the beneficial waters of the Nile and its annual cycles.

[117] Guardian of the east, one of the founders of the Zodiac.

[118] Guardian of the west, regarded as "he who refreshes his brothers."

[119] See Abraham 1:3-4 [1:8-14]).

[120] Hugh Nibley argued the practice existed in Egypt, and sacrifice of virgins from the royal household was a reaction to drought (see Nibley, *Abraham in Egypt*, supra, pp. 177-178; 231-232; 336-339). He links it to the Egyptian Sed festival, "the moment at which the king, overcome by the evil power of Seth, lies helpless on the couch, which is simultaneously deathbed, embalming table, and bed of deliverance and rejuvenation. In actual practice the person on the couch was a substitute for the king and was really sacrificed; according to the legends, Abraham was chosen to be such a substitute, and after his miraculous delivery (the priest being killed in his place with the overthrow of the altar), he also took the king's place in sitting upon his throne" (ibid., p. 80).

Abraham is not credible.[121] But the book is not set in Egypt. Human sacrifice is known to have taken place in the land of the Chaldeans where the Abraham account is actually based. *Newsweek* reported the following:

> Archaeologists have uncovered evidence that at least 11 children and young people were killed as a result of ritualistic sacrifice between 3100 and 2800 B.C.E. Their research was published Wednesday in the journal Antiquity. …Some remains show evidence of stab wounds, but researchers aren't sure how all of the individuals lost their lives. One male had violent injuries to his hip and head, similar to wounds reconstructed from other Mesopotamian ritual sacrifices. …"It is unlikely that these children and young people were killed in a massacre or conflict," the London Natural History Museum's Brenna Hassett said in a statement. "The careful positioning of the bodies and the evidence of violent death suggest that these burials fit the same pattern of human sacrifice seen at other sites in the region."[122]

This discovery puts Chaldean human sacrifice occurring at or near the conventional dating of Abraham's life.

The *New York Times* reported on human sacrifices at an ancient location named "Ur" located in Iraq:

> A new examination of skulls from the royal cemetery at Ur, discovered in Iraq almost a century ago, appears to support a more grisly interpretation than before of human sacrifices associated with elite burials in ancient Mesopotamia, archaeologists say.
>
> Palace attendants, as part of royal mortuary ritual, were not dosed with poison to meet a rather serene death. Instead, a sharp instrument, a pike perhaps, was driven into their heads.

---

[121] See Kerry Muhlestein and John Gee's article defending early Egyptian human sacrifice and arguing it continued into the Middle Kingdom during Abraham's lifetime (*An Egyptian Context for the Sacrifice of Abraham*, Journal of Mormon Studies, Volume 20, Number 2, 2011). They use three examples.
[122] Katherine Hignett, *Newsweek*: "Ancient Mesopotamia: Ritual Child Sacrifice Uncovered in Bronze Age Turkey," June 29, 2018.

Archaeologists at the University of Pennsylvania reached that conclusion after conducting the first CT scans of two skulls from the 4,500-year-old cemetery. The cemetery, with 16 tombs grand in construction and rich in gold and jewels, was discovered in the 1920s. A sensation in 20th century archaeology, it revealed the splendor at the height of the Mesopotamian civilization.

The recovery of about 2,000 burials attested to the practice of human sacrifice on a large scale. At or even before the demise of a king or queen, members of the court – handmaidens, warriors and others – were put to death. Their bodies were usually arranged neatly, the women in elaborate headdress, the warriors with weapons at their side.[123]

According to the Book of Abraham, none of the names of Chaldean gods—or any of the religious practices Abraham witnessed and experienced—were Egyptian. They were cultic practices and may have been entirely conducted in a locality that imitated their own incorrect understanding of the religion of Egypt. Chaldea's Ur was populated by 'Egyptophiles' who were apparently imitating and practicing a local corruption of an ancient Egyptian religion.[124] They clearly got some things about the Egyptian religion wrong (and may have gotten very many things wrong).

Robert Ritner's book includes a chapter written by Christopher Woods addressing the location of Ur. The chapter is titled, "The Practice of Egyptian Religion at 'Ur of the Chaldees'?"[125] The chapter begins by acknowledging that, "The location of 'Ur of the Chaldees'...remains open for debate."[126] He explains, "Cuneiform sources attest a number of settlements bearing the name of Ur (or a name phonetically similar) in northern Syria, southeastern Turkey,

---

[123] John Noble Wilford, *New York Times*, "At Ur, Ritual Deaths That Were Anything but Serene," Oct. 26, 2009.

[124] Their departures from authentic Egyptian religious practices is a reminder to us that Napoleonic-era Egyptophiles may have likewise poorly reconstructed the Egyptian language using the Rosetta Stone. If both groups of Egyptophiles erred, then we rely on them at the peril of making similar wrong conclusions.

[125] See Ritner, Robert K. *The Joseph Smith Egyptian Papyri: A Complete Edition*, supra, pp. 73-74.

[126] Ibid., p. 73.

and northern Mesopotamia, mostly small villages, and so making for unlikely candidates for biblical Ur."[127]

A discovery of an ancient library of thousands of cuneiform tablets in 1975 raised another possible location for Abraham's Ur, this new one being located in ancient Haran rather than a thousand miles away, as previously thought.[128]

Since the Ritner book is a collection of scholarly criticism of the Book of Abraham, the author does not leave it open-ended. Instead, he speculates Ur may have been at a specific Babylonian location. Based on that assumption, he concludes, "If we are correct in identifying Abraham's Ur with Babylonian Ur, this poses grave difficulties for the account given in the Book of Abraham."[129] Obviously, if the author is not correct, the inverse is also true and should acknowledge: If we are incorrect in identifying Abraham's Ur with Babylonian Ur, then we don't know anything about this matter, and it poses no justifiable difficulty for the account in the Book of Abraham.

Hugh Nibley discusses Ur in *An Approach to the Book of Abraham*[130] from pages 424 to 428. He writes on page 427:

> What leaves the door wide open to discussion is the existence in western Asia of a number of different Urs. Ur in the south was a great trade center once, and since Abraham was a merchant, one should expect to find him there. But on the other hand that same Ur had founded merchant colonies far to the north and west at an early date, and some of those settlements, as was the custom, bore the name of the mother city. (Citations and footnotes omitted)

The angel of God rescued Abraham from being sacrificed on the altar. The angel killed the priest attempting to sacrifice Abraham.

---

[127] Ibid., p. 74. He does not explain why a small location could not be, or is unlikely to be, the actual Biblical site.

[128] "...there is another city specifically called 'Ur in Haran.' 'An especially intriguing notice,' write the editors of the Biblical Archaeology Review, 'is a reference to "Ur *in* Haran."' Does this mean that the Ur from which Abraham originally came was near Haran rather than a thousand miles further away in southern Mesopotamia where "Ur of the Chaldees," is supposedly located?'" (Nibley, *Abraham in Egypt*, supra, p. 85, italics in original).

[129] Ibid.

[130] Deseret Book, 2009, edited by John Gee.

This resulted in *great mourning in Chaldea...* (Abraham 2:1 [1:20]). Following this, *a famine prevailed throughout all the land of Chaldea* (ibid., vs. 4 [1:30]). During the famine in Ur of Chaldea, the Lord commanded Abraham to leave, and the events in the Book of Abraham finally move away from Ur: *Now the Lord had said unto me, Abram, get yourself out of your country, and from your kindred, and from your father's house, unto a land that I will show you. Therefore, I left the land of Ur of the Chaldees, to go into the land of* **Canaan** (ibid., vs. 5 [2:3-4], emphasis added). The story moves but is still not **in Egypt**–nor is Abraham **heading** to Egypt in the account.

The next location must have been comparatively uninhabited when Abraham's family arrived. They name the location after Abraham's deceased brother, Haran. Abraham explains his family went *unto the land which* **we** *denominated Haran* (ibid., emphasis added). It apparently had no name before their arrival, since they denominated (or named) the place. We have no way to identify the location but only know it was away from the earlier (also unknown) location called Ur.

At Haran, there is no mention of famine. Abraham's father, Terah, had repented of his idolatry in Ur, but in Haran he returned to it. When God later told Abraham to depart from Haran, Terah remained behind.[131]

Abraham's journey then takes him through Jershon in the land of Canaan.[132] There–**still not in Egypt**–Abraham built an altar. Moving on again, he arrives in Sechem, *situated in the plains of Moreh* at a place described as *the borders of the land of the Canaanites* (Abraham 4:2 [2:18]). He is still not in Egypt. In that location the Lord promised Abraham, *unto thy seed I will give* **this** *land* (ibid. [2:19], emphasis added). Abraham was **not** given Egypt.

Famine is mentioned again in the land given to Abraham's seed, and as a consequence of that, Abraham reports: *I, Abraham, concluded to go down into Egypt, to sojourn there, for the famine became very grievous* (ibid., vs. 3 [2:21]). Abraham's conclusion to go down to Egypt confirms for us that he had not yet reached Egypt during **any part** of his account to that point.

---

[131] See Abraham 2:5-3:1 [2:1-11].
[132] See Abraham 4:1 [2:14-16].

Abraham received a great revelation about the stars, the heavens, events among the pre-existing spirits of mankind, the fall of Satan, and the Creation of this world. This great revelation comprises the remainder of Abraham's account in his book. However, the account clearly states that God told Abraham: *I show these things unto you, **before** you go into Egypt* (Abraham 5:4 [3:15], emphasis added). Accordingly, **nothing** in the Book of Abraham took place in Egypt. When it is added into the Genesis account, what happened following the conclusion of the Book of Abraham text is: *And it came to pass that when Abram had come into Egypt...* (Genesis 7:4 [12:14]) and goes on from there to explain about Sarai being accosted.

Willard Richards' introduction that claims the book is "purporting to be the writings of Abraham **while he was in Egypt**" is demonstrably wrong from the text itself–32 times the Book of Abraham states otherwise. When **nothing** in the text reckons from Egypt, it is questionable how useful criticism is of the Book of Abraham from an Egyptological vantage point. We should expect there to be some deviations from Egyptian religion, language, or culture in the book. The account only covers events among ancient people, in an uncertain location called "Ur," located somewhere in Chaldea. Those people were only imitative of Egypt. They were not Egyptians. And the events in the book did not happen "while [Abraham] was in Egypt."

One hieroglyph appears in all three Facsimiles:

- It is figure 10 in Facsimile 1,
- At the bottom and adjacent to the figure 2 in Facsimile 2, and
- Figure 3 in Facsimile 3.

The hieroglyph is used to represent "Abraham in Egypt."[133] The figure is a libation table (or "traditional offering stand"[134]) on which drink and food were offered. Since Abraham concluded to travel to Egypt because of famine,[135] a symbol of drink and food for Abraham in Egypt would be altogether apt. But the table figure shows a lotus

---

[133] Facsimile 1 identifies the figure as "Abraham in Egypt." Facsimile 2 does not deal directly with the figure but mentions a revelation in which Abraham learned about the Creation while he was offering sacrifice on an altar at an undefined time and place. Facsimile 3 identifies the figure as "Signifies Abraham in Egypt, referring to Abraham as given in Figure 10 of Facsimile No. 1."

[134] Ritner, *The Joseph Smith Egyptian Papyri*, supra, p. 93.

[135] See Abraham 4:3 [2:21].

flower atop it. The lotus was a symbol of ascent to the throne of God. That concept is most clearly referenced in the explanation of panel 2 of Facsimile 2.[136] It is at least thought-provoking that Joseph identified the food and drink offering stand and a symbol of ascending to God to be representing Abraham's presence in Egypt.

To be clear, because nothing in the Book of Abraham happened in Egypt, it is questionable how useful anything authentically Egyptian (if we are able to determine that) is to understand or to question that text. The names and practices Abraham encountered imitated—but did not correctly replicate—the religion of 9th Dynasty Egypt. The text explains that the place where Abraham was offered as human sacrifice is an unknown village located somewhere under Chaldean influence named "Ur." However, Ur could have been in any Mesopotamian location across thousands of square miles from Turkey, northern Syria, into Iraq, or Iran.[137] There are many known villages contemporary with Abraham known to have been named "Ur."[138] Of course, there may have been many others unknown to us with the same or similar name. The text ends before Abraham enters Egypt, and therefore, the continuation of an account involving Abraham picks up in Genesis. This begins halfway through Genesis 7:4. That account deals only briefly with the "princes" bringing Sarai to Pharaoh who was then plagued because of Sarai's presence. Pharaoh then returns Sarai to Abram, at which point Abram and Sarai were sent away.[139]

Because nothing in the Book of Abraham or Genesis gives any detail about Abraham's experiences in Egypt, we have no narrative account to help give context to the facsimiles. We do not know if Facsimile No. 3–like Facsimile No. 1–is a scene that took place outside of Egypt. The footnotes explaining the scene end with this clarification: *Abraham is reasoning upon the principles of astronomy in the king's court.*[140] It is unclear which "king's court" is being referenced.

---

[136] That panel has this explanation: "...near to the celestial or place where God resides; holding the key of power also pertaining to other planets, as revealed from God to Abraham as he offered sacrifice upon an altar which he had built unto the Lord" (Book of Abraham, Facsimile 2, figure 2).

[137] There is an Old Babylonian inscription that mentions a place named "Ulishim" that is very similar to the Book of Abraham's mention of "Olishem" (see Abraham 1:3 [1:8-11] and Ritner, *The Joseph Smith Egyptian Papyri*, supra, p. 74).

[138] "Several of these—Ura, Ura's, Uram, Uri'um, Urru and Ura—are encountered in the Elba archives dating from the mid-third millennium" (ibid.).

[139] See Genesis 7:4-5 [12:11-20].

[140] These are the last words beneath the facsimile and refer to the entire scene.

Clearly, the people of Ur involved in Abraham's experiences imitated Egypt. They sought to imitate the Egyptian "earnest imitation." Therefore, we cannot be certain if Facsimile No. 3 is reporting an event that took place among people who imitated Egyptian religious rites or if they instead happened in Egypt. If it is the former, it is consistent with the rest of the text where nothing else has Abraham in Egypt.

The Book of Abraham explains the Egyptian Pharaoh could only imitate the Holy Order but had no right to claim that priestly position.[141] In context, this exposes the Chaldean's error in looking to Egypt for Divine governance. These Urian residents even anointed for themselves a *priest of Pharaoh* (Abraham 1:2 [1:7]) who practiced human sacrifice. Was this an innovation by Ur or imitative of an Egyptian rite? We do not know anything certain about the "Ur" mentioned in the Book of Abraham. But we know it was distant from (and only imitating) an Egyptian imitation of the religion of the Fathers. We only have Abraham's understanding of what these people were up to.

It is clear from the text that "before" his journey "into Egypt," Abram was shown a great revelation about the pre-existence, Creation, and organization of the stars. It raises the question of where Abraham tried to clear up the people's understanding in Facsimile No. 3. Was it in Ur, in Haran, among the Canaanites, or with the Egyptians? If it is something that happened in Egypt, then it is the only thing in the Book of Abraham that took place in Egypt.[142]

The Book of Abraham clarifies many "mysteries" that are not otherwise to be found in Scripture. But Scriptures tell us there are many important truths that are withheld from us. Even if they are unknown to us, there are "mysteries" still part of the true religion first revealed to Adam.

We learn of God's promise to the righteous in T&C 69:2 [76:7-10]:

---

[141] See Abraham 2:3 [1:25-28].
[142] Ritner includes H. Michael Marquuardt's chapter, "Joseph Smith's Egyptian Papers: A History" in his opus, which acknowledges the text is about "what took place prior to Abraham's going to Egypt" (Ritner, *The Joseph Smith Egyptian Papyri*, supra, p. 34).

> *Unto them will I reveal all my mysteries, yea, all the hidden mysteries of my kingdom. From days of old and for ages to come will I make known unto them the good pleasure of my will, concerning all things to come. Yea, even the wonders of eternity shall they know, and things to come will I shew them, even the things of many generations. Their wisdom shall be great and their understanding reach to Heaven, and before them the wisdom of the wise shall perish and the understanding of the prudent shall come to naught. For by my spirit will I enlighten them and by my power will I make known unto them the secrets of my will, yea, even those things which eye has not seen, nor ear heard, nor yet entered into the heart of man.*

We are told in Alma 9:3 [12:9-10] that those who give heed and are diligent are rewarded with understanding:

> *It is given unto many to know the mysteries of God; nevertheless, they are laid under a strict command that they shall not impart – only according to the portion of his word which he doth grant unto the children of men, according to the heed and diligence which they give unto him. And therefore, he that will harden his heart, the same receiveth the lesser portion of the word. And he that will not harden his heart, to him is given the greater portion of the word, until it is given unto him to know the mysteries of God, until they know them in full.*

While Christ was among the Nephites, the greatest part of what He taught them is withheld from our record. We read in 3 Nephi 9:5 [19:31-32]:

> *He went again a little way off and prayed unto the Father, and tongue cannot speak the words which he prayed, neither can be written by man the words which he prayed. And the multitude did hear, and do bear record, and their hearts were open, and they did understand in their hearts the words which he prayed.*

There are many other references in Scripture to important things that are left out of our canon. The true religion contains many "mysteries" that are important, not yet known or taught, but which were to be restored to the faithful at the end.

The Book of Abraham helps us uncover some of the missing information about the religion of the first Fathers. The first verse of the Book of Abraham includes these remarkable words:

> *I sought for the blessings of the Fathers and the right whereunto I should be ordained to administer the same. Having been myself a follower of righteousness, desiring also to be one who possessed great knowledge, and to be a greater follower of righteousness, and to possess a greater knowledge, and to be a Father of many nations, a prince of peace, and desiring to receive instructions and to keep the commandments of God, I became a rightful heir, a high priest, holding the right belonging to the Fathers. It was conferred upon me from the Fathers: it came down from the Fathers, from the beginning of time, yea, even from the beginning (or before the foundations of the earth) to the present time, even the right of the firstborn (or the first man – who is Adam – or first Father) through the Fathers unto me. I sought for my appointment unto the Priesthood according to the appointment of God unto the Fathers concerning the seed.* (Abraham 1:1 [1:2-4])

Abraham begins by explaining that he "sought for the blessings of the Fathers," the very thing Malachi prophesies will return before the great and dreadful return of the Lord. Abraham obtained what will be available again. Those blessings of the Fathers will be administered again before the end.

At the beginning of his record, Abraham mentions some of the specific things that are part of "the blessings of the Fathers." This identifies Abraham, not Joseph Smith, as the writer of the book.

When the Holy Order is established in its fullness, there is one Patriarchal head appointed to stand as the husbandman-father, occupying the same position as the first Father (or Adam). When God set Adam at the head, "The tasks given to Adam are of a priestly nature: caring for sacred space. In ancient thinking, caring for sacred space was a way of upholding creation. By preserving order, non-order was held at bay."[143] This priestly responsibility was what Abraham sought. He explained that he wanted to *possess a greater knowledge, and to be a Father of many nations, a prince of peace, and desiring to receive instructions and to keep the commandments of God, I became a rightful heir, a high priest, holding the right belonging to the Fathers* (ibid.). The Lord offered to return this lost fullness in Joseph Smith's day,[144]

---

[143] John H. Walton, *The Lost World of Adam and Eve*, IVP Academic 2015, p. 106.
[144] See T&C 141:10 [D&C 124:25-28].

but the required conditions were not met.[145] Therefore, the fullness was not "restored again" and remains unrestored.[146]

Abraham knew more about the Holy Order in his day than Joseph in 1842. After all, Abraham had the records of the Fathers. Much of what Joseph learned about the Holy Order (or as he termed it, the "fullness of the priesthood") appears to have come as a result of him translating the Book of Abraham.[147]

Abraham knew Adam was the Father of many nations. Likewise, the first Patriarchs all expected to have numerous posterity and to be Fathers of many nations. The line of the Patriarchs named in Scripture is a list of those through whom the Holy Order descended and does not name all of the righteous. The residue of righteous was also blessed. The original Holy Order meeting at Adam-Ondi-Ahman is described in Scripture:

> *Three years previous to the death of Adam, he called Seth, Enos, Cainan, Mahalalel, Jared, Enoch, and Methuselah, who were all high priests, with the residue of his posterity who were righteous, into the valley of Adam-Ondi-Ahman, and there bestowed upon them his last blessing.* (T&C 154:19 [D&C 107:53])

Those names are listed in order from Adam (who was the first to hold the presiding Patriarchal position) to the youngest holding that right.

The Holy Order in its fullness is a right of government or right of dominion. Anciently, it was always held in a line of descent. Abraham marks the first time that a non-direct lineal descendant was sealed in the Holy Order to hold it in its fullness. Once sealed, Abraham was entitled to become a *Father of many nations, ...a rightful heir, ...holding the right belonging to the Fathers"* (Abraham 1:1 [1:2]).

---

[145] See T&C 141:11,13-14 [D&C 124:29-48]. For a discussion of this, see Chapter 10, "The Temple at Nauvoo" in *Passing the Heavenly Gift*, (Millcreek Press, 2011), pp. 265-287.

[146] For a discussion of this, see Chapter 11, "The Priesthood was Taken From Israel" in *Passing the Heavenly Gift*, supra, pp. 288-317.

[147] For example, Nauvoo era sermons discuss concepts of pre-Earth existence and organizing the Creation, salvation for the dead, eternal covenants, eternal progression, being added upon in successive probations, and temple covenants that relate to the Book of Abraham text. It is unlikely the April 7, 1844 "King Follett Discourse" would have been possible without the 1842 completion of the Book of Abraham.

This right is **not worldly**. Abraham's record gives us a perfect vantage point to understand the difference between worldly government and the government of God. At the time of Abraham, any earthly king did not have the right to make that claim. The Pharaoh of Abraham's day feigned to hold it, claiming it descended to him through Noah. Abraham explained the conflict:

> *Pharaoh, being a righteous man, established his kingdom and judged his people wisely and justly all his days, seeking earnestly to imitate that order established by the fathers in the first generations, in the days of the first Patriarchal reign, even in the reign of Adam, and also Noah, his father, who blessed him with the blessings of the earth, and with the blessings of wisdom, but cursed him as pertaining to the Priesthood. Now Pharaoh being of that lineage by which he could not have the right of Priesthood, notwithstanding the Pharaohs would fain claim it from Noah through Ham, therefore my father was led away by their idolatry.* (Abraham 2:3 [1:26-27])

Pharaoh was "righteous" but still descended from a line that could not claim legitimate rule. He modeled his kingdom after the order established by the first Fathers, but it could only be an imitation. He claimed a lineal connection with Noah, which was true enough, but his ancestry gave him no heavenly acknowledgment for his rule.[148] And because he descended from a line that usurped authority not given to them by God, all those who submitted to his earthly rule practiced idolatry.

Abraham, on the other hand, was given dominion, the right to rule over nations, patriarchal status, and the rights belonging to the Fathers. But Abraham made no attempt to displace the Pharaoh. They were rivals, to be sure, but Abraham was content to hold the right, receive instructions, be a diligent follower of righteousness, be one who possessed great knowledge, be a greater follower of righteousness, and to possess a greater knowledge. He was content to teach his followers the path of righteousness. Unlike Pharaoh, he

---

[148] Nibley identifies the lineal defect as being matriarchal: "He nonetheless traced his descent and his throne to 'a woman, who was the daughter of Ham, the daughter of Egypt' (Abraham 1:23); this woman 'discovered the land' and 'settled her sons in it' (Abraham 1:24). Her eldest son became the first pharaoh, ruling 'after the manner' of the patriarchal order (Abraham 1:25), which the king sought earnestly to 'imitate.' Thus the government of Egypt was carried on under the fiction of being patriarchal while the actual line was matriarchal, the queen being 'the wife of the God and bearer of the royal lineage'" (*Abraham in Egypt*, Deseret Book, 2000, p. 428, citations to the LDS version of the Book of Abraham).

did not assert authority over others. Abraham was interested in eternity and not earthly recognition and control. Hugh Nibley described the circumstance:

> The Book of Abraham brings out the main points of rivalry between the patriarch and the pharaoh in high relief: Each claims to possess the only true priesthood and with it the only true kingship. The earliest legends of Egypt and Mesopotamia introduce us to a scene repeated over and over again in apocalypses and testaments of the patriarchs, prophets, and apostles, of a great and terrible monarch who feels his divinity threatened and his dominion challenged by an emissary of the true God.[149]

Nibley has observed that "Pharaoh was always unsure of his authority over his own people."[150] There were many Pharaohs in later dynasties who investigated their claim to authority.

> Of particular interest are those devout and sincere pharaohs who spent their days in the archives engaging in the constant search of Egyptian rulers for divine authority, such men as King Neferhotep in the Thirteenth Dynasty, the great Amenophis I, "a wise and inspired man," according to Manetho, who yearned to see the gods but feared to risk any force or trickery to get his wish, or Ptolemy the son of Glaucias, "the recluse of the Serapeum," spending all his days in the library, as does the hero of the Setne Khamuas story, searching in the House of Life for the book that bestows the knowledge of divine dominion and authority.
>
> The trouble was that they lacked revelation. In Egypt, Henri Frankfort observed, "The actions of individuals lacked divine guidance altogether."[151]

Egypt's claims may seem arrogant after the Exodus of Israel. However, their civilization attempted to preserve something precious. As one writer put it, "Ancient Egyptians inherited their

---

[149] *Abraham In Egypt*, Deseret Book, 1981, 2000, p. 254.
[150] Ibid., p. 233.
[151] Ibid.

great wisdom from a much earlier Elder culture which was able to pass on the flame of knowledge before its own apparent demise."[152]

God has declared His intent to assert control over His Creation and overthrow all governments. The Christmas 1832 revelation states:

> *And thus with the sword and by bloodshed, the inhabitants of the earth shall mourn. And with famine, and plague, and earthquake, and the thunder of heaven, and the fierce and vivid lightning also, shall the inhabitants of the earth be made to feel the wrath, and indignation, and chastening hand of an Almighty God, until the consumption decreed has made a full end of all nations, that the cry of the saints, and of the blood of the saints, shall cease to come up into the ears of the Lord of Sabaoth*[153] *from the earth, to be avenged of their enemies.* (T&C 85:3 [D&C 87:6-7])

All nations, other than the Holy Order family-government ordained by God, will be brought to a full end. Or in the various iterations of the prophecy of Malachi, God *will smite the earth with a curse* (Malachi 1:12; [4:6]), or *the whole earth would be utterly wasted at his coming* (JSH 3:4 [D&C 2:3]). This doesn't mean universal death. It means universal dissolution into chaos with no governance possible, apart from the one that He intends to establish that will provide revelation, guidance, order, and preserve **His people**. The only surviving rule or dominion at that time will be the one tied to the Fathers. It will be the people whose one heart is like the one heart of the Fathers.[154] They will possess the promises made to the Fathers, or in other words, they will have been sealed to the Fathers. It is phrased differently in different versions of Malachi's prophecy, but they all mean the same thing. Occasionally, God describes the same thing in different words. The purpose is to help us grasp His meaning.

There are many obstacles to overcome before the Lord returns in glory. Recovering the religion of the Fathers, becoming of one heart with the Fathers, and fulfilling the prophecy of Malachi are directly connected to Abraham. In a very real sense, it will not happen without a connection to Abraham.

---

[152] *Gods of Eden*, supra, p. 17.
[153] The term is a reference to the "hosts of heaven" or Elohim.
[154] In Egypt, the "heart" was the seat of knowledge.

Holding the promises made to Abraham is not just a covenant. It also involves knowledge. Joseph Smith was required to recover the "fullness of the scriptures" (or translate the Bible as it was in the bosom of the Lord) into a volume for the faithful to study. Joseph warned the Latter-day Saints that they would fall without the fullness.[155] Until the publication of the Restoration Edition of the Scriptures, there was no version of the fullness of the Scriptures available. Of course, they do not accomplish anything if they are not read and studied.

Repenting and reclaiming the fullness of the Scriptures was a required first step of repentance for the Restoration to continue. When that step was taken, there was a covenant. If people are faithful to the covenant, the Restoration will continue.

Abraham was not content with knowledge. He wanted to obtain greater knowledge. The purpose of pursuing knowledge was to receive and obey commandments. Greater knowledge facilitates greater obedience. Knowledge is not the goal, it is the desirable effect that knowledge has on the heart and mind of a righteous soul.

Knowledge about the Holy Order can be misused. Even **understanding** its rights has inspired envy, jealousy, and anger. Cain murdered Abel because Cain understood the importance of standing at the head of the Holy Order. As he contemplated the possibility of it slipping away from him, Satan tempted him to usurp the right by murdering the more worthy heir. The account of that attempted overthrow is succinct:

> *Satan says unto Cain, Swear unto me by your throat, and if you tell it, you shall die. And swear your brethren by their heads and by the living God that they tell it not, for if they tell it, they shall surely die – and this that your father may not know it. And this day I will deliver your brother Abel into your hands. And Satan swore unto Cain that he would do according to his commands. And all these things were done in secret. And Cain says, Truly I am Mahon, the master of this great secret – that I may murder and get gain; wherefore, Cain was called Master Mahon. And he gloried in his wickedness. And Cain went into the field and Cain talked with Abel his brother. And it came to pass*

---

[155] "God had often sealed up the Heavens because of covetousness in the church. Said the Lord would cut his work short in righteousness and except the church receive the fullness of the scriptures they would yet fall" (JSP, *Documents, Volume 2: July 1831–January 1833*, p. 85).

> *that while they were in the field, Cain rose up against Abel his brother and slew him. And Cain gloried in that which he had done, saying, I am free; surely the **flocks** of my brother fall into my hands.* (Genesis 3:9 [Moses 5:29-33], emphasis added)

The "flocks of my brother" were not sheep; they were posterity. Abel was to become Adam's successor and stand as the Father of many nations. By displacing Abel, Cain hoped to be next in the line of Patriarchal Fathers.

Ether chapter 4 shows how the envy of "kingship" results in generations of murderers obtaining power through bloodshed. The Holy Order is not a worldly thing. It cannot be severed from the Powers of Heaven or the Heavenly Council. The presiding Patriarch of the Holy Order is a representative of the Heavenly Council who lives as a mortal on Earth. This is why the Patriarchal head of the Holy Order is the shepherd for the faithful, husbandman for the Creation, and teacher responsible for dispensing Divine knowledge. That was who **Adam was** and what **Abraham became**.

The Holy Order is approved for practice in a proper, functioning temple belonging to God.[156] As Walton put it:

> When we consider the Garden of Eden in its ancient context, we find that it is more sacred space than green space. It is the center of order, not perfection, and its significance has more to do with divine presence than human paradise.[157]

> ...We did not lose paradise as much as we forfeited sacred space and the relationship it offered, thereby damaging our ability to be in relationship with God and marring his creation with our own under-developed ability to bring order on our own in our own wisdom.[158]

---

[156] It can be restored by opening the heavens, but once restored, it is perpetuated in the sacred space of a Holy Temple. Although Abraham had the records of the Fathers and the heavens open, he was still required to receive ordination rites from Melchizedek before obtaining the Holy Order. "Abraham says to Melchizedek, I believe all that thou hast taught me concerning the priesthood and the coming of the Son of Man; so Melchizedek ordained Abraham and sent him away. Abraham rejoiced, saying, Now I have a priesthood" (*TPJS*, p. 322-323 [August 27, 1843]).

[157] *The Lost World of Adam and Eve*, supra, p. 116.

[158] Ibid., p. 145.

What records that remain do not give a full picture of how much was anciently included in God's temple. For example, Margaret Barker's investigation has uncovered an ancient presence of the Divine Mother who was identified as "Wisdom." She explained that Josiah's reform changed the First Temple by removing, rejecting, and deducting:[159]

> Wisdom was eliminated, even though her presence was never forgotten, the heavenly ascent and the vision of God were abandoned, the hosts of heaven, the angels, were declared to be unfit for the chosen people, the ark (and the presence of Yahweh which it represented) was removed, and the role of the high priest was altered in that he was no longer anointed. All of these features of the older cult were to appear in Christianity.[160]

Later Christianity, like Josiah's reforms, also abandoned these parts of the religion. Joseph Smith never had the opportunity to finish restoring them. How oft would God have gathered people together under the arms of the Holy Order,[161] but mankind has not been willing or even interested.

We see one tragic example of this in Exodus 18:5 [34:1-3]:

> And the Lord said unto Moses, Hew two other tablets of stones, like unto the first, and I will write upon them also the words of the law, according as they were written at the first on the tablets which you broke. But it shall not be according to the first, for I will take away the Priesthood out of their midst. Therefore, my Holy Order and the ordinances thereof shall not go before them, for my presence shall not go up in their midst lest I destroy them. But I will give unto them the law as at the first; but it shall be after the law of a carnal commandment, for I have sworn in my wrath that they shall not enter into my presence, into my rest, in the days of their pilgrimage. Therefore, do as I have commanded you, and be ready in the morning, and come up in the morning unto Mount Sinai, and present yourself there to me in the top of the mount. And no man shall come up with

---

[159] One of the hallmarks of apostasy is deduction, subtraction, and forgetting.
[160] *The Great Angel*, p. 15.
[161] See, e.g., 3 Nephi 4:9 [10:3-7]; T&C 29:8 [D&C 43:23-26].

you, neither let any man be seen throughout all the mount, neither let the flocks nor herds feed before that mount.[162]

When the Powers of Heaven are offended, the spirit is grieved, the Powers withdraw, and the Holy Order rites are either not restored or, if restored, come to an end.[163] Cain's ambition could not be accomplished through any degree of unrighteousness. It was doomed from the time the plan was suggested by Satan. Yet Abel was murdered, and a conspiracy to seize power by blood and horror began while Adam was alive. Mankind is no less ambitious today. That impulse to exercise control, dominion, and compulsion persists and can be seen everywhere: in business, churches, governments, and schools.

The reason so little is understood about the Holy Order is because weak men aspire to honors. Once they learn about the Order, they want control over it.[164] Therefore, it is withdrawn from mortal men from time to time.[165] When not active among men, it only remains present through John the Beloved. John was translated, acting thereafter only as an angelic minister. Because of this, he is not free

---

[162] The significance of this to ancient Israel is explained in T&C 82:12-14 [D&C 84:19-25]: "And this greater Priesthood administers the gospel and holds the key of the mysteries of the kingdom, even the key of the knowledge of God. Therefore, in the ordinances thereof, the power of godliness is manifest, and without the ordinances thereof, and the authority of the Priesthood, the power of godliness is not manifest unto man in the flesh, for without this no man can see the face of God, even the Father, and live. Now, this, Moses plainly taught to the children of Israel in the wilderness, and sought diligently to sanctify his people that they might behold the face of God, but they hardened their hearts and could not endure his presence. Therefore, the Lord, in his wrath (for his anger was kindled against them) swore that they should not enter into his rest – which rest is the fullness of his glory – while in the wilderness. Therefore, he took Moses out of their midst, and the Holy Priesthood also."

[163] "The rights of the Priesthood are inseparably connected with the Powers of Heaven and that the Powers of Heaven cannot be controlled nor handled, only upon the principles of righteousness. That they may be conferred upon us, it is true, but when we undertake to cover our sins or to gratify our pride, our vain ambition, or to exercise control, or dominion, or compulsion, upon the souls of the children of men in any degree of unrighteousness, behold, the Heavens withdraw themselves, the spirit of the Lord is grieved, and when it is withdrawn, Amen to the priesthood or the authority of that man"(T&C 139:5 [D&C 121:36-37]).

[164] Too often when men learn some great truth and recognize it by the spirit, they then assume that confers upon them some authority or right to act. Nothing could be further from the truth. There is a great gulf between learning and recognizing and authority to act.

[165] See, e.g., T&C 82:12-14 [D&C 84:19-28].

to openly preside.¹⁶⁶ The Lord explained to Peter concerning John: *I will make him as flaming fire and a ministering angel. He shall minister for those who shall be heirs of salvation who dwell on the earth . . .* (JSH 13:19 [D&C 7:6]). John has ministered only "as a flaming fire and a ministering angel," which circumscribes **how** and to **whom** his ministry is extended. He ministers "for those who shall be heirs of salvation who dwell on the earth," or (as Moroni explained by quoting his father):

> *The office of their ministry is to call men unto repentance, and to fulfill and to do the work of the covenants of the Father which he hath made unto the children of men, to prepare the way among the children of men by declaring the word of Christ unto the chosen vessels of the Lord, that **they** may bear testimony of him; and by so doing, the Lord God prepareth the way that the residue of men may have faith in Christ, that the holy ghost may have place in their hearts.* (Moroni 7:6 [7:31-32], emphasis added)

Angels, including John, minister to chosen vessels. It is the responsibility of **mortal** ministers to preach the message. The message must be accepted and acted on for faith in Christ. The Holy Order must be held again by mortals and must be returned voluntarily back to Christ in a second Adam-ondi-Ahman.¹⁶⁷ That is the arrangement made before the foundation of the Earth. Christ gave dominion over the Earth to Adam, and Christ will receive back the right of dominion before His return in glory.

All knowledge can be misused. The more the Holy Order is understood, the more sobering it becomes. Greater knowledge is being employed today to abuse, control, and subjugate people. The

---

¹⁶⁶ As explained by Joseph Smith in a *Times & Seasons* editorial, "Peter could baptize, and angels could not, so long as there were legal officers in the flesh holding the keys of the kingdom, or the authority of the priesthood" (*JSP, Documents, Volume 11*, p. 30).

¹⁶⁷ Joseph Smith explained, "Adam-Ondi-Ahman...is the place where Adam shall come to visit his people, or the Ancient of Days shall sit, as spoken of by Daniel the prophet" (T&C 132:1). This assembly at the end is a mirror of the meeting that took place between the Lord, Adam, and his righteous posterity three years previous to Adam's death (see T&C 154:19). "Father Adam, Michael, he will call his children together and hold a council with them to prepare them for the coming of the Son of Man. He (Adam) is the father of the human family, and presides over the spirits of all men, and all that have had the keys must stand before him in this grand council. . . .The Son of Man stands before him, and there is given him glory and dominion. Adam delivers up his stewardship to Christ, that which was delivered to him as holding the keys of the universe, but retains his standing as head of the human family" (*TPJS*, p. 157).

Scriptures warn of *evils and designs which will exist in the hearts of conspiring men in the last days* (T&C 89:2 [D&C 89:4]). Any advantage one individual holds over another can be improperly used to subjugate, oppress, and exploit. Therefore, the hidden mysteries that reach into the highest heaven and contemplate the darkest abyss[168] will include knowledge capable of misuse. Mysteries are guarded, cloaked in sacred ritual, confined to a qualified[169] group of trusted and proven initiates.

The Holy Order will return lost knowledge to the Earth. The specifics have been withheld from Scripture, but the scope of that knowledge has been referred to often. Abraham had the records of the first Patriarchs, and he described some of what was included in the sacred texts:

> *But the records of the Fathers, even the Patriarchs, concerning the right of Priesthood, the Lord, my God, preserved in my own hands. Therefore, a knowledge of the beginning of the creation, and also of the planets and of the stars, as they were made known unto the Fathers, have I kept even unto this day.* (Abraham 2:4 [1:31])

Knowledge to be revealed through the Holy Order will include information about the beginning of this Creation. At the beginning, "The order that God brought focused on people in his image to join with him in the continuing process of bringing order, but more importantly on the ordering of the cosmos as sacred space."[170] We disturb this Creation because we are disorderly. We are the opposite of what God intended for us.

> ...human sin has blocked God's purposes for the whole creation; but God hasn't gone back on his creational purpose, which was and is to work in his creation through human beings, his image-bearers. In his true image-bearer, Jesus the Messiah, he has rescued humans from their sin and death in order to reinscribe his original purposes, which include the extension of sacred space into all creation, until the earth is

---

[168] "Your mind, O man, if you will lead a soul unto salvation, must stretch as high as the utmost Heavens, and search into and contemplate the lowest considerations of the darkest abyss, and expand upon the broad considerations of eternal expanse. You must commune with God" (T&C 138:18).

[169] The word "qualified" is used to mean approved by revelation from God, not a "recommend" interview conducted by a man.

[170] *The Lost World of Adam and Eve*, supra, p. 150.

indeed full of God's knowledge and glory as the waters cover the sea. God will be present in and with his whole creation; the whole creation will be like a glorious extension of the tabernacle in the wilderness or the temple in Jerusalem.[171]

Restoring the Holy Order will add knowledge about the religious significance of the planets and stars. They were ordained as "signs" to establish "seasons."[172] That does not just mean times of the year but also times of dispensations, ministries, and judgments.

The gospel of Christ and the mysteries of His kingdom are vast. The doctrine of Christ is succinct. The entire doctrine of Christ is set out in one paragraph of Third Nephi.[173] Christ was emphatic that His brief statement of His doctrine is solely and exclusively all of it and there can be nothing added to it. He warns us:

> *Whoso shall declare more or less than this, and establisheth it for my doctrine, the same cometh of evil and is not built upon my rock, but he buildeth upon a sandy foundation, and the gates of hell standeth open to receive such when the floods come and the winds beat upon them.* (3 Nephi 5:9 [11:40])

But the records of the first Patriarchs handed down to Abraham include the Creation, a discussion of planets and stars, and "greater knowledge."[174] The reason so much more was revealed and preserved in the records of the Fathers is because the gospel of Christ **includes all truth.**[175]

From the Scriptures, it is clear many of those involved with the Holy Order–as well as dispensation heads and prophets–were taught truth far beyond the doctrine of Christ.

Enoch, for example, was given seership by the Lord and through it uncovered hidden things:

> *And the Lord spoke unto Enoch, and said unto him, Anoint your eyes with clay and wash them, and you shall see. And he did so. And he*

---

[171] Ibid., p. 176.
[172] See Genesis 2:6 [Moses 2:14]; Abraham 7:5 [4:14].
[173] See 3 Nephi 5:9 [11:31-39].
[174] Joseph Smith knew these subjects would be included in the Restoration (see T&C 138:21 [D&C 121:26-32]).
[175] See T&C 138:24.

> beheld the spirits that God had created, and he beheld also things which were not visible. And from that point forward came the saying abroad in the land, A **seer** has the Lord raised up unto his people. (Genesis 4:3 [Moses 6:35-36], emphasis added)

Enoch was shown all eternity by the Lord:

> The Lord spoke unto Enoch and told Enoch all the doings of the children of men. Wherefore, Enoch knew and looked upon their wickedness and their misery, and wept, and stretched forth his arms. And he beheld eternity, and his bowels yearned, and all eternity shook. (Genesis 4:18 [Moses 7:41])

The Lord showed Moses everything about this world:

> And it came to pass that Moses looked and beheld the world upon which he was created. And as Moses beheld the world, and the ends thereof, and all the children of men who are and who were created, of the same he greatly marveled and wondered. (Genesis 1:2 [Moses 1:8])

The Brother of Jared saw everything through the ends of the Earth:

> He shewed unto the brother of Jared all the inhabitants of the earth which had been, and also all that would be. And the Lord withheld them not from his sight, even unto the ends of the earth. For the Lord had said unto him in times before that if he would believe in him, that he could shew unto him all things, it should be shewn unto him. Therefore, the Lord could not withhold anything from him, for he knew that the Lord could shew him all things. (Ether 1:15 [3:25-26])

From these few Scriptures, we learn that Enoch, Moses, the Brother of Jared, and Abraham learned or experienced:

- Knowledge about the spirits God created,
- Things not visible to the eye of mankind,
- All the doings of mankind,
- Beholding eternity,
- The creation of this world and the end thereof,
- All the inhabitants of the world past, present, and future, and
- All things.

Others had many "mysteries" revealed to them. Remember that *knowledge of the mysteries of godliness is obtained only through **obedience** to God* (T&C 159:31, emphasis added). That is why Abraham's desire to get additional knowledge was so he could receive instructions and keep God's commandments.[176] Obedience earns more knowledge, and more knowledge requires greater obedience. They move together in one eternal round.

In one sense, the religion of the Fathers is based on a direct connection to God. Reduced to one thought, it is that as long as God is speaking directly to a body of people,[177] giving them commandments, they have the most essential element of the religion of the Fathers. If they remain true to that connection, all things can be restored to them.

The last-days' people of Zion will have more revelation and, consequently, more commandments than others. Disobedient souls who refuse to obey God's commandments have no interest in Zion. Likewise, they have no opportunity for seeing Zion, because it is only possible through receiving commandments and obeying them. This has been explained in modern scripture:

> *Yea, blessed are they whose feet stand upon the land of Zion, who have obeyed my gospel, for they shall receive for their reward the good things of the earth, and it shall bring forth in her strength. And they also shall be crowned with blessings from above, yea, and with commandments not a few, and with revelations in their time, they that are faithful and diligent before me.* (T&C 46:1 [D&C 59:3-4])

This is a critical part of Christ's gospel. Any body of saints in any age of the world must obtain the Lord's commandments addressed to them to be saved. Commandments given to others belong to them, and only commandments God gives to us belong to us. Joseph Smith explained this matter, after referring to the New Testament:

> And though we cannot claim these promises which were made to the ancients for they are not our property, merely

---

[176] See Abraham 1:1 [1:1-4].

[177] Although individuals may receive revelation, the first Father's religion requires God's commandments to be given for a body of people. Adam and Eve lost Eden and God's presence. Thereafter, the purpose was to regain "Eden" (or God's presence), which was achieved in the City of Zion in Father Enoch's day, then again in Salem in Father Melchizedek's day.

because they were made to the ancient Saints, yet if we are the children of the Most High, and are called with the same calling with which they were called, and embrace the same covenant that they embraced, and are faithful to the testimony of our Lord as they were, **we** can approach the Father, in the name of Christ as they approached Him, and for ourselves obtain the same promises. These promises, when obtained, if ever by us, will not be because Peter, John, and the other Apostles…walked in the fear of God and had power and faith to prevail and obtain them; but it will be because **we, ourselves**, have faith and approach God in the name of His Son Jesus Christ, even as they did; and when these promises are obtained, they will be promises **directly to us**, or they will do us no good. They will be communicated for **our** benefit, being our own property (through the gift of God), earned by our own diligence in keeping His commandments, and walking uprightly before Him.[178]

This is affirmed in our Scriptures:

> *I admit that by reading the scriptures, of truth, the saints in the days of Paul could learn, beyond the power of contradiction, that Abraham, Isaac, and Jacob had the promise of eternal life confirmed to them by an oath of the Lord; but that promise or oath was no assurance to them of their salvation, but they could, by walking in the footsteps and continuing in the faith of their fathers, obtain for **themselves** an oath for confirmation that they were meet to be partakers of the inheritance with the saints in light.*

> *If the saints in the days of the apostles were privileged to take the ancients for examples, and lay hold of the **same** promises, and attain to the **same** exalted privilege of knowing that **their** names were written in the Lamb's Book of Life and that **they** were sealed there as a perpetual memorial before the face of the Most High, will not the same faithfulness, the same purity of heart and the same faith bring the same assurance of eternal life, and that in the same manner, to the children of men now in this age of the world?*

---

[178] *Teachings of the Prophet Joseph Smith*, Deseret Book, 1972, p. 66; *Documentary History of the Church, Volume 2*, Deseret Book, 1976, pp. 21-22; *JSP, Documents, Volume 3*, pp. 483-484, emphasis added. Both *TPJS* and *DHC* give the date for this written instruction from Joseph Smith as January 22, 1834, but the *JSP* dating is March 1834. The *JSP* dating is the correct one.

> *I have no doubt but that the holy prophets and apostles and saints in ancient days were saved in the kingdom of God; neither do I doubt but that they held converse and communion with him while they were in the flesh, as Paul said to his Corinthian brethren that the Lord Jesus showed himself to above five hundred saints at one time after his resurrection. Job said that he knew that his Redeemer lived and that he should see him in the flesh in the latter days. I may believe that Enoch walked with God and by faith was translated. I may believe that Noah was a perfect man in his generation and also walked with God. I may believe that Abraham communed with God and conversed with angels. I may believe that Isaac obtained a renewal of the covenant made to Abraham by the direct voice of the Lord. I may believe that Jacob conversed with holy angels, and heard the voice of his Maker, that he wrestled with the angel until he prevailed and obtained the blessing. I may believe that Elijah was taken to Heaven in a chariot of fire with fiery horses. I may believe that the saints saw the Lord and conversed with him face to face after his resurrection. I may believe that the Hebrew church came to Mount Zion, and unto the city of the living God, the Heavenly Jerusalem, and to an innumerable company of angels. I may believe that they looked into eternity and saw the Judge of all, and Jesus the Mediator of the new covenant. But will all this purchase an assurance for **me**, and waft **me** to the regions of eternal day, and seat **me** down in the presence of the King of kings with my garments spotless, pure, and white?*
>
> *Or must I not rather obtain for myself, by my own faith and diligence in keeping the commandments of the Lord, an assurance of salvation **for myself**? And have I not an equal privilege with the ancient saints? And will not the Lord hear **my** prayers and listen to **my** cries as soon as he ever did to theirs, if I come to him in the manner they did?* (T&C 99:14-17, emphasis added)

Whatever the status other believers may have today, there are promises that have been given by God directly to us. There are now more revelations and more commandments than at any other time. Beginning with the "Answer to the Prayer for Covenant" and the accompanying Covenant, God has given new commandments.[179] If they are followed, the promises made to this people will increase in light and truth until the perfect day.[180] We are not reading the

---

[179] The list of commandments that follows has been gathered from T&C 157, 158, 159, 173, and 176.
[180] See T&C 36:4 [D&C 50:17-24].

promises made by God to other people, because we have God's commandments and promises given to us.

The commandments given directly by God include, but are not limited to, the following:

- God's will is to have us love one another, but we lack the ability to respectfully disagree with each other. The Lord compares us to Paul and Peter whose disagreements resulted in jarring and sharp contentions. We have been commanded to do better.

- Wisdom counsels us to align our words with our hearts, but we refuse to take counsel from Wisdom. There have been sharp disputes between us that should have been avoided.

- Satan is a title and means accuser, opponent, and adversary; hence, once he fell, Lucifer became (or in other words, was "called") Satan because he accuses others and opposes the Father. The Lord rebuked Peter and called him Satan because he was wrong in opposing the Father's will, and Peter understood and repented. We sometimes act as Satan: accusing one another, wounding hearts, and causing jarring, contention, and strife through accusations. Rather than loving one another, some have dealt unkindly–as if they were the opponents, accusers, and adversaries. In this, we have been wrong, and the Lord has rebuked us for our error.

- We have the duty to bind the spirit of the accuser (Satan) within us so that we give no heed to accuse others. It is not enough to say we love God; we must also love our fellow man. Nor is it enough to say we love our fellow man while we–as Satan–divide, contend, and dispute against any person who labors on an errand seeking to do God's will.

- How we proceed must be as noble as the cause we seek. We are commanded to end our unkind and untrue accusations against one another and make peace.

- We have been warned that even a single soul who stirs up the hearts of others to anger can destroy the peace of the Lord's people. All must **equally** walk in God's path, not only to profess but to **do** as professed.

- As a people, we honor with our lips, but our hearts are corrupt, filled with envy and malice, returning evil for good, sparing none (even those with pure hearts among us) from our unjustified accusations and unkind backbiting.

- We are commanded to repent and bring forth fruit showing repentance.

- It is not enough to receive God's covenant, but we must also abide its requirements.

- Without the fruit of repentance and a broken heart and a contrite spirit, we cannot keep the Lord's covenant. We are commanded to be like our Lord who is meek and lowly of heart.

- We have scarred one another by our unkind treatment of each other, and we bear the scars on our countenances, from the soles of our feet to the head, and every heart is faint. Our visages have been so marred that our hardness, mistrust, suspicions, resentments, fear, jealousies, and anger toward our fellow man bear outward witness of our inner self; we cannot hide it. When the Lord appears to us, instead of confidence, we feel shame. We fear and withdraw from the Lord because we bear the blood and sins of our treatment of our brothers and sisters. We are commanded to come to our Lord, and He will make sins as scarlet become white as snow and will make us stand boldly before Him, confident of His love.

- We are commanded to forgive one another, to be tender with one another, pursue judgment, bless the oppressed, care for the orphan, and uplift the widow in her need–for the Lord has redeemed us from being orphaned and taken us that we are no longer a widowed people. We are told to rejoice in the Lord and rejoice with our brethren and sisters and to be one.

- We are forbidden from letting our hearts remain divided from one another and divided from the Lord.

- We are commanded to be of one heart and regard one another with charity.

- We have been commanded to measure our words before giving voice to them and to consider the hearts of others. Although a man may err in understanding concerning many things, if we regard one another with charity, then our brother's error in understanding will not divide us.

- We are commanded to study to learn how to respect our brothers and sisters and to come together by **precept, reason,** and **persuasion**, rather than sharply disputing and wrongly condemning each other, causing anger. God warns us to take care how we invoke His name.

- God has cautioned us that a great work remains yet to be done. His covenant requires that we abide in it (not as in the former time when jarring, jealousy, contention, and backbiting caused anger, broke hearts, and hardened the souls of those claiming to be His saints during Joseph Smith's life, but we are commanded to receive it in spirit, in meekness, and in truth).

- We are commanded to forgive all men. If we forgive men their trespasses, our Heavenly Father will also forgive us; but if we forgive not men their trespasses, neither will our Heavenly Father forgive our trespasses.[181]

- We cannot be at peace with one another if we take offense when none is intended. We are commanded to not judge others except by the rule we want used to weigh ourselves.

- We are to let our pride and our envy and our fears depart from us.

- He has asked us to covenant with Him to cease to do evil and to seek to continually do good.

- God's covenant with us requires we receive the Scriptures approved by the Lord as a standard to govern us in our daily walk in life, for us to accept the obligations established by the Book of Mormon as a covenant, and to use the Scriptures to correct ourselves and to guide our words, thoughts, and deeds.

---

[181] See also Matthew 3:30 [6:1415]; 3 Nephi 5:34 [13:9-15]; T&C 175:41.

- We are commanded to assist all others (who covenant to likewise accept the scriptural standard to govern their lives) to keep the Lord's will, to succor those who stand in need, to lighten the burdens of our brothers and sisters whenever we are able, and to help care for the poor among us.

- God has asked us, by covenant, to seek to become of one heart with those who seek the Lord to establish His righteousness.

- We are commanded to teach our children to honor the Lord and to seek to recover His lost sheep and teach them of the Lord's ways, to walk in them.

- We have been instructed that tithes of this people are to be used for the poor.

- We are commanded to love one another and to labor willingly alongside each other.

- God instructed us to trust His words and proceed always in faith, believing that **with Him** all things **are** possible.

- We have been commanded to stop murmuring and complaining against all who labor, because the Lord is pleased with all those who are grateful and merciful and who will have Him as their God.

Consider the question posed by the Lord to us: *What have you learned? What ought you to have learned?*[182] The Lord's question **is still pending**. It seems apparent to me that these questions are designed to make us talk to one another.

There is a gulf between knowledge and wisdom. We may have access to greater knowledge, but we often display very little wisdom. Knowledge can be arrogant. Wisdom is humble. Knowledge inflates our pride, but wisdom cautions us that we are still very far from being godly people.

Great spiritual development by individuals in isolation will never equip the individual to fit into a spiritually-developed society. Alone, we seek connection to God. God represents the highest ideal

---

[182] These questions are posed twice in T&C 176:2 and again in 176:12.

in compassion, acceptance, and kindness. It is easy to make a place for God in our hearts. But other people are not always compassionate, easy to accept, or kind. God is pure, and mankind is not. When called "good" by the rich young man, Christ responded, *Why do you call me good? None is good save one, that is God* (Luke 10:9 [18:19]). If Christ would not allow Himself to be called "good," then there is little reason to call one another "good."

Individual spiritual development and group spiritual development are two very different challenges. Recent revelations focus on the development of a **group**. Everything points to God's desire to have His **people** turn to Him and live in harmony with one another. It is clear the Lord's objective is Zion and not merely to make us better individuals.

There is a Buddhist story about an enlightened monk who lived near a city having difficulties and conflicts. People from the town asked the monk to come into town to guide them so they could resolve their conflicts, but he refused. He preferred living alone and meditating. The town sent more representatives to ask again, and the monk refused again. Finally, a great crowd of people went to ask the monk for his help because, without it, they said they could never reach peace. At last, he relented. On the way back to town, in the joyful crowd, an old woman stumbled into the monk, pushing him to the ground. This made him very angry.

It is far easier for a hermit to live in quiet meditation than to live in harmony within a community. We are called into a dispensation with **more expected** than individual salvation and enlightenment. For the salvation of souls today, the primary focus of God's religion is to **gather a community**. God's purpose for the end times is focused on making people of one heart and one mind.

Context for the Book of Abraham
Part 2

God's spirit is withdrawing from the world. In the Covenant of Christ Conference on September 3, 2017, we were told:

> Those who have entered faithfully into the covenant this day are going to notice some things. The spirit of God is withdrawing from the world. Men are increasingly more angry without good cause. The hearts of men are waxing cold. There is increasing anger and resentment of gentiles. In political terms, it's rejection of white privilege.
>
> Language of scriptures gives a description of the events now underway and calls it the end of the times of the gentiles. This process with the spirit withdrawing, will end on this continent, as it did with two prior civilizations in fratricidal and genocidal warfare. For the rest of the world, it will be as in the days of Noah in which, as that light becomes eclipsed, the coldness of men's hearts is going to result in a constant scene of violence and bloodshed. The wicked will destroy the wicked.
>
> The covenant, if it is kept, will prevent you from losing light and warmth of heart as the spirit now steadily recedes from the world. The time will come when you will be astonished at the gulf between the light and truth **you** will comprehend and the darkness of mind of the world.[183]

We have seen astonishing increases since September 3, 2017 of darkness, lies, deceit, and conflict. Lies can imprison people. The chain Enoch saw that Satan had over the world[184] was constructed of lies. The "chains of darkness" that hold men in prison after death are also lies.[185] Today those chains of darkness hold fast many people,

---

[183] See "Closing Remarks," Covenant of Christ Conference, transcript, *Restoration Archives*, Boise, Idaho, 2017, www.restorationarchives.com, emphasis added.

[184] "And behold, the powers of Satan were upon all the face of the earth. And he saw angels descending out of Heaven, and he heard a loud voice saying, Woe, woe unto the inhabitants of the earth. And he beheld Satan, and he had a great chain in his hand, and he veiled the whole face of the earth with darkness; and he looked up and laughed, and his angels rejoiced" (Genesis 4:15 [Moses 7:24-26]; see also Alma 9:1 [12:1-6]).

[185] Ibid., v. 21 [Moses 7:54-57]; see also T&C 22:2 [D&C 38:5-6].

and their numbers are growing. *Woe unto them that call evil good and good evil, that put darkness for light and light for darkness, that put bitter for sweet and sweet for bitter* (Isaiah 1:17 [5:20]). Confusion over what is light and what is dark and the difference between sweet and bitter comes from widespread lies being accepted as truth.

As the light of Heaven withdraws, it is all the more important for us to keep it within us. But we also have many "thinking errors." Recent revelations from God make it clear we are **being challenged to be fit to live in peace with one another**. The Scriptures tell us we should see God in our fellow man.

On His way to Jerusalem to be sacrificed, Jesus was asked by a rich young man,

> *Which is the first commandment of all? And Jesus answered him, The first of all the commandments is: Listen, and hear, O Israel, the Lord our God is one Lord. And you shall love the Lord your God with all your heart, and with all your soul, and with all your mind, and with all your strength. This is the first commandment. And the second is like this: You shall love your neighbor as yourself. There is no other commandment greater than these.* (Mark 5:44 [12:28-31])

Why would love of your neighbor[186] as yourself be compared to the commandment to love God with all your heart, soul, might, and mind? It is because God is in every person you will ever meet. All life is a gift from God. God loans us the breath of life:

> *God who has created you, and has kept and preserved you, and has caused that ye should rejoice, and has granted that ye should live in peace one with another – I say unto you that if ye should serve him who has created you from the beginning, and art preserving you from day to day by lending you breath that ye may live, and move, and do according to your own will, and even supporting you from one moment to another...* (Mosiah 1:8 [2:20-21])

God sustains us **all** from moment to moment. Through His power, we live and move. If God is sustaining every living person from one moment to another, then God is within all of us.[187] If He loves them

---

[186] Even those with whom we have serious religious disagreements are our "neighbors" (see Luke 8:7-8 [10:25-37]).
[187] See "Understanding Your Soul," *Restoration Archives*, Sandy, Utah, 2021, www.restorationarchives.com.

enough to support them, lend them breath, give them power to move and do according to their will, sustaining their life continuously, how can we hate them?

There are sincere people who pray and ask God questions, and they get answers. Often the answers given to one might be different than the answer given to another. Both believe they have intelligence from God and desire to stay true to the answer they have received. In these circumstances, are conflicts inevitable? Of course. But does that mean harmony is impossible? Of course not.

This conflict is like another Buddhist story about a monk who accompanied a great teacher to learn how to help others. Throughout the day, the monk listened as the teacher gave answers to those who came for help. At the end of the day, the monk was disappointed and told the teacher his answers contradicted one another. The teacher had told one to do the opposite of what another was told. It made no sense to the monk. The teacher replied that there is only one road, but those who depart to the left must be guided back to the right. And those who departed to the right must be guided back to the left. The road does not change, but finding it after it has been lost depends on where the individual has wandered away.[188]

What does it mean for us when there is a contradiction between God's answer to one prayerful soul and His answer to another prayerful soul? If discussion is warranted, it means that by talking through their disagreements, they may both be guided back to the one path to be followed. Sometimes that discussion will take time, experience, and careful, solemn thoughts. Even if the communicating takes a great while, why rush through a process that is designed to bring greater understanding? What if conversation does not produce an agreement? There is nothing wrong with tabling a discussion that has not reached everyone's approval and then resuming the discussion another day. Why the rush?

---

[188] It is also like driving directions from downtown Salt Lake to Brigham Young University in Provo. It requires a series of direction changes (sometimes left, sometimes right) and moving westward to Interstate 15, then south, but reversing and going eastward at the Orem diagonal. Unless the person receiving directions is willing to accept the many course changes, they will not arrive at the destination. It does them no good to notice and reject the apparent "contradictions" in the directions, because they will reliably guide them to the intended location.

In legal disputes, there is a conflict resolution process called "mediation." Mediation involves a third-party mediator who helps the parties reach a settlement. The overwhelming majority of mediated cases reach settlement. However, I've seen many cases fail to reach a resolution, and the parties walk away from the mediation table still in conflict. But later, after the parties have taken the time to reflect on the mediation, most of those unresolved cases will eventually settle as well.

I think the "Answer to the Prayer for Covenant" is the Lord **pleading with us** to take the time to **talk through our differences**. There is nothing in those words of counsel that requires us to quickly resolve matters. Quite the opposite. The "Answer" is filled with instruction to us about the **process**, leaving the result to be obtained eventually—through a respectful process, no matter how much time may be needed. To the extent the Lord cares about time at all, He warns us against "haste."[189]

The "recommended means" to reach harmony are *persuasion, by long-suffering, by gentleness and meekness, and by love unfeigned, by kindness and pure knowledge, which shall greatly enlarge the soul;* **without hypocrisy** *and* **without guile***...* (T&C 139:6 [D&C 121:41-42], emphasis added).

During the Scriptures project, there were many conflicts and differences to resolve. These conflict's resolutions delayed the project **far** beyond what any of us thought it would take. When the two independent groups were first combined, both groups thought their respective project was complete (or nearly so). But it was quickly apparent that the projects differed, and there were issues to resolve. It took months, and when all believed the end was approaching again, new source material and new research was uncovered that required more than half the project to begin again.

More than a year after expected conclusion, the project continued. At one point, I sent an email expressing my view of how I hoped to conduct myself:

> *I would rather submit to the decision of the group than insist that my view be followed. For me, harmony between brethren is more important than getting what I think best to be followed. I believe*

---

[189] See T&C 45:13 [D&C 58:54-57]; 47:3,5 [60:8-9,12-15]; 50:6 [63:22-24]; 58:2 [133:7-15]; 101:15-16 [101:67-75]; 102:4; and 149:3.

> harmony can lead to much greater things than can merely enforcement of even a correct view. I know how difficult it is to have a correct view, because of how often I have been corrected by the Lord. Sometimes I am humiliated by my foolishness when the Lord reproves me. Humiliation can lead to humility, but my experience is that the humiliation is accompanied by shame, whereas humility can proceed with a clear conscience.
>
> My experience with others leads me to conclude that if we can have one heart first, eventually we can likewise come to have one mind. But if we insist on having one mind at the outset, we may never obtain one heart together.[190]

A friend of mine sent me a Facebook rant from a man who wants to teach others and very much demands attention and respect. His angry rant ended by telling those who were insufficiently respectful of his great writings that they were "hypocrites and pollutions, and unless you fall down before God in humility, you will suffer horrors you can't imagine. …The greater the reasons you resist, the more you will be damned." The approach reminded me of the enlightened hermit monk who became angry once jostled.

Zion cannot be established in solitary meditation. It requires a community. And community requires us to see God in one another. It requires we listen to and understand one another. That cannot happen if we do not talk with each other about even difficult subjects and serious disagreements. The sharper the disagreement, the more we need to learn! As the Lord explained, *There have been sharp disputes between you that should have been avoided. I speak these words to **reprove** you that you may **learn**, not to upbraid you so that you mourn. I want my people to have understanding* (T&C 157:5, emphasis added). Those may be some of the greatest words God has ever condescended to give to any people, at any time–and we treat them as if they're a rebuke for someone else and not ourselves, as if we needn't heed them.

We have also been taught:

> Study to learn how to respect your brothers and sisters and to come together by precept, reason, and persuasion, rather than sharply

---

[190] The email was adopted by the committee and vote of the conference to be the "Epigraph" for the Teachings and Commandments.

disputing and wrongly condemning each other, causing anger. Take care how you invoke my name. Mankind has been controlled by the adversary through anger and jealousy, which has led to bloodshed and the misery of many souls. Even strong disagreements should not provoke anger, nor to invoke my name in vain as if I had part in your every dispute. Pray together in humility and together meekly present your dispute to me, and if you are contrite before me, I will tell you my part. (Ibid., vs. 54)

From the foregoing, it is clear that the Lord has, in His mercy, chosen to speak again. God has renewed His covenant and provided commandments. But His instructions and commandments are to guide a community into godly harmony. It is only possible to rise up to become that community by following the instructions of God.

I am ashamed of every conflict I have caused. I regret any discourtesy I have shown to another. But I do not recall ever demanding someone submit to me. At every turn, I have intended only to persuade and invite, not demand and insist. I am no one's commander, president, or church authority. You cannot make me anything more than your equal, because I refuse to rise above anyone else. We are all fellow-servants (and, often, unprofitable ones at that).

It is important to God that the Book of Mormon has been accepted as a covenant.[191] It is a bond between God and man. God has made for Himself a people and "numbered us among the House of Israel."[192] But remember that Israel has a long history of rebellion, disobedience, and rejection. Those who remain faithful and obedient to God are those who will vindicate His prophecies, covenants, and promises. Among other things, the people who keep His covenant will be called upon to build the tabernacle where He will take up His abode on Earth in the New Jerusalem.[193] On July 14, 2017, He gave this revelation:

Whenever I have people who are mine, I command them to build a house, a holy habitation, a sacred place where my presence can dwell or where the Holy Spirit of Promise can minister, because it is in such a place that it has been ordained to recover you, establish by my word

---

[191] See T&C 158:3,9-10.
[192] See T&C 156:15; 157:48; 158:10.
[193] See Genesis 4:22 [Moses 7:58-64].

> and my oath your marriages, and endow my people with knowledge from on high that will unfold to you the mysteries of godliness, instruct you in my ways, that you may walk in my path. And all the outcasts of Israel will I gather to my house, and the jealousy of Ephraim and Judah will end; Ephraim will not **envy** Judah and Judah will not **provoke** Ephraim. (Ibid., vs. 41, emphasis added)

Knowledge that will unfold the mysteries of godliness and instruct in God's path is designed to be embedded in the House of God. At this point, the prophecy waiting to be fulfilled states:

> ...when the mountain of the Lord's house shall be established in the top of the mountains, and shall be exalted above the hills, and all nations shall flow unto it. And many people shall go and say, Come and let us go up to the mountain of the Lord, to the house of the God of Jacob, and he will teach us of his ways and we will walk in his paths. For out of Zion shall go forth the law ... (Isaiah 1:5 [2:2-3])[194]

The first Fathers had teachings and beliefs that included much more than what has been preserved from Joseph's day. We should expect greater information to be passed along to us. But knowledge without the tempering presence of wisdom will prove to be dangerous. Aspiring and ambitious men are unwise. They cannot be trusted.

There are those who think circumcision originated with Abraham through his covenant with God.[195] That was a **restoration** of circumcision, **not the origination** of it. In the beginning, when a son of Adam and a daughter of Eve covenanted to marry, the son of Adam shed blood by circumcision in order to seal the marriage covenant. Once healed, the marriage was consummated, at which point the virgin daughter of Eve shed blood to complete the sealing of the marriage covenant. Insomuch as Abraham and Sarah had been married for many years prior to the covenant, it was ordained that circumcision for all of Abraham's descendants would take place at eight days.[196] Because of the restoration of the covenant—and God adapting it for Abraham and all the faithful who would follow him as their Father—circumcision was expected to be done at birth. This **remains an obligation** for all the righteous.

---

[194] See also Micah 1:9 [4:1-8].
[195] See Genesis 7:30 [17:10-14].
[196] See Genesis 7:29 [JST 17:8-12]; Acts 4:3 [7:1-10].

The much later Law of Moses perpetuated the Abrahamic practice of circumcision at eight days.[197] Even non-Israelites who wanted to observe the Passover were required to be circumcised to participate in the Paschal meal.[198] Although the Law of Moses is no longer in effect, restoring circumcision through Abraham pre-dates Moses by nearly seven centuries and is still in effect.[199] Fulfilling and ending the Law of Moses did nothing to change the earlier covenant with Abraham and his descendants.

There were other practices known to the first Fathers that have been lost. We should expect to learn the earliest worship was not limited to a "Father in Heaven" but included a Divine Family. I have already addressed this subject in "Our Divine Parents."[200] The first Patriarchs understood there to be a Father, Mother, and Divine Son who were all recognized as Divine. There was also a Heavenly Council or Divine Counsel who were among a recognized "hosts of heaven" who also held positions of authority.

In addition to a Sabbath day of rest, the first Fathers were given three Divinely appointed religious festivals or holidays (more correctly, "Holy Days") that were to be observed yearly. These were tied to the Creation to remind mankind of God's wisdom and mercy in organizing this world for mankind.

Because of apostasy, numerous other festivals or religious observances have been added by men. For example, the Jews added Hanukkah,[201] Purim,[202] and Yom HaShoah.[203] Christians added Lent,[204] Ash Wednesday,[205] and Christmas[206] (among others). When

---

[197] See Leviticus 4:1 [12:1-5].

[198] See Exodus 8:7 [12:43-51].

[199] See T&C 140:21. If the original practice originating at the time of Adam is considered, it predates the Law of Moses by several millennia.

[200] This talk is available on www.restorationarchives.com, as a download on www.denversnuffer.com, and in *Eight Essays*, Mill Creek (2019), beginning on p. 270.

[201] A festival commemorating the rededication of the Second Temple in Jerusalem at the time of the Maccabean Revolt.

[202] A holiday commemorating the saving of the Jewish people from Haman, an Achaemenid Persian Empire official who was planning to kill all the Jews, as recounted in the Book of Esther.

[203] Observed as a Jewish commemoration for the approximately six million Jews who perished in the Nazi Holocaust.

[204] Lent was added in the 4th Century to mark the 40-day period that ends on Easter.

[205] A fast day that begins the 40-day period of Lent.

[206] A mid-winter celebration intended to mark the birth of Christ but set on the calendar to coincide with the pre-Christian Roman observance of Sol Invictus.

the original religion returns, the original religious festivals–always centered in a sacred site or temple–will also return.

I mentioned that before Abraham entered Egypt, he received a great revelation about the stars, the heavens, events among the pre-existing spirits of mankind, the fall of Satan, and the Creation of this world. This list summarizes part of the knowledge associated with the Holy Order; God wanted the husbandman, shepherd, and High Priest to comprehend:

- Why this Creation was organized,

- Man's position in the cosmos,

- Who the "hosts of heaven" were,

- That there was a cosmic rebellion in the heavens,

- That a cosmic covenant was established that framed the Creation, established conditions for mankind to gain experience, and through which mankind could progress, and

- That all things in nature–including the light of the sun, moon, planets, and stars– were purposefully organized and governed by a covenant with God.

Abraham–like Adam (at the beginning) and his descendant, Enoch–was caught up into Heaven and received a tutorial endowment from God. The purpose was simple enough: helping each of them to understand what came before and what comes after this life. This was to help rescue them from death and hell. In a very real sense, the curriculum of the Holy Order is designed to give both a **personal** and a **cosmic** context to Christ. The Holy One of Israel is the redeeming Messiah who has been our constant Protector, Example, and Guide from the foundation of Creation.

The Messiah was the central figure in the Creation. The Messiah was the foremost figure opposing the rebellion in the Heavens. The Messiah came to save the Creation by His self-sacrifice. Man's universal death is reversed by their universal resurrection, made possible by the Messiah. And it will be the Messiah who judges mankind and will assign them to various conditions following mortality.²⁰⁷ It is the Messiah who occupies the central position in all the mysteries of godliness. The members of the Holy Order understood this best and, therefore, were most trusted to preach, teach, testify, minister, and watch over the posterity of Adam (and later, the posterity of Abraham).

The most useful and obedient servants of the Lord have been those who have been exposed to the greatest understanding of His eternal role. The opening paragraph of Abraham's book is a direct statement of the relationship between knowledge and obedience.²⁰⁸

From the first generation, the Patriarchs used ritual to convey a great body of information (a theatrical revelation) to initiates. The Book of Abraham itself appears to be a ritual text.²⁰⁹

> ...the book of Abraham, far from being merely a diverting or edifying history, is a discourse on divine authority, which also is the theme of the three facsimiles. The explanations to the three plates make it perfectly clear that they are meant as diagrammatic or formulaic aids to an understanding of the subject of priesthood on earth.²¹⁰

Enoch's account (now in Genesis of the Restoration Edition Scriptures) also appears to be a ritual text.²¹¹ Hugh Nibley calls Enoch:

> ...the great initiate who becomes the great initiator.²¹²

---

²⁰⁷ See, e.g., Acts 6:7 [10:34-43]; Romans 1:9,70 [2:12-16; 14:10-12]; 2 Timothy 1:10 [4:1-8]; 2 Nephi 11:6 [25:16-19]; Mosiah 1:15 [3:10-13]; 8:14 [16:6-12]; Alma 8:16 [11:42-44]; and Mormon 3:4 [6:16-22].

²⁰⁸ See also Lectures on Faith 7:19, "It was by obtaining a knowledge of God that men got all things which pertain to life and godliness, and this knowledge was the effect of faith." Joseph explained on April 10, 1842, "A man is saved no faster than he gets knowledge, for if he does not get knowledge, he will be brought into captivity by some evil power in the other world, as evil spirits will have more knowledge, and consequently more power than many men who are on the earth. Hence it needs revelation to assist us, and give us knowledge of the things of God."

²⁰⁹ See Hugh Nibley, "Abraham's Temple Drama," *The Temple in Time and Eternity*, FARMS, Provo (1999); also the chapter by David Calabro, "The Choreography of Genesis: The Book of Abraham as a Ritual Text," *Sacred Time, Sacred Space, & Sacred Meaning: The Temple on Mount Zion Volume 4*, (The Interpreter Foundation and Eborn Books, 2020).

²¹⁰ Nibley, *An Approach to the Book of Abraham*, p. 178.

²¹¹ See, e.g., Hugh Nibley, *Enoch the Prophet*, (Deseret Book 1986), pp. 19-21; Jeffrey M. Bradshaw, *The LDS Story of Enoch as the Culminating Episode of a Temple Text*, BYU Studies, Vol. 53, No. 1, 2014, p. 38.

²¹² Nibley, *Enoch the Prophet*, p. 19.

He adds,

> His is the independent intelligence always seeking further light and knowledge. He is the great observer and recorder of all things in heaven and earth, of which God grants him perfect knowledge. The great learner, he is also the great teacher: Enoch the Initiator into the higher mysteries of the faith and secrets of the universe; Enoch the Scribe, keeper of the records, instructor in the ordinances, aware of all times and places, studying and transmitting the record of the race with intimate concern for all generations to come. He offers the faithful their greatest treasure of knowledge. He is the seer who conveys to men the mind and will of the Lord.[213]

The religion of the Fathers cannot be adequately conveyed if it is separated from ritualized knowledge. By using symbol, movement, gesture, dress, architecture, sound, orientation, and setting, it is possible to embed light and truth in a way to engage the mind, spirit, and heart of mankind. The temple can **be** the house in which it is possible to stretch the mind of man both upward and downward by the things presented there.[214] "The temple itself was but a copy of the heavenly temple, the liturgy on earth a shadow of the worship of the angels."[215] It is through covenant-forming ordinances—including rituals—that the power of Godliness has been manifest to mankind.[216] *The order of the House of God has and ever will be the same, even after Christ comes, and after the termination of the thousand years it will be the same, and we shall finally roll into the Celestial Kingdom of God and enjoy it forever* (T&C 117:4).

---

[213] Ibid., p. 21.

[214] Margaret Barker wrote: "The holy of holies was outside time, and so those who entered looked out from beyond time and saw history as a whole. ...the whole history of the world on the reverse side of the veil: '[Everything] whether done or to be done in the time to come, till the end of time, were all printed on the curtain of the Omnipresent One'; and when Jesus told people of his experiences in the wilderness, he said that he had seen 'all the kingdoms of the world in a moment of time' (Luke 4:5 [KJV])" (*Temple Mysticism: An Introduction*, SPCK Press 2011, pp. 45-46, quoting 3 Enoch 45:6).

[215] Barker, *The Great Angel*, supra, p. 118.

[216] "And this greater Priesthood administers the gospel and holds the key of the mysteries of the kingdom, even the key of the knowledge of God. Therefore, in the ordinances thereof, the power of godliness is manifest, and without the ordinances thereof, and the authority of the Priesthood, the power of godliness is not manifest unto man in the flesh, for without this no man can see the face of God, even the Father, and live" (T&C 82:12 [D&C 84:19-22]).

When writing from a dungeon in Missouri, Joseph Smith's reflection on what is needed to save souls clarifies the function of a temple:

> ...because the things of God are of deep import, and time, and experience, and careful and ponderous and solemn thoughts can only find them out. Your mind, O man, if you will lead a soul unto salvation, must stretch as high as the utmost Heavens, and search into and contemplate the lowest considerations of the darkest abyss, and expand upon the broad considerations of eternal expanse. You must commune with God. ...None but fools will trifle with the souls of men.
>
> How vain and trifling have been our spirits, our conferences, our councils, our meetings, our private as well as public conversations: too low, too mean, too vulgar, too condescending for the dignified characters of the called and chosen of God, according to the purposes of his will from before the foundation of the world, to hold the keys of the mysteries of those things that have been kept hid from the foundation until now, of which some have tasted a little, and which many of them are to be poured down from Heaven upon the heads of babes, yea, the weak, obscure, and despisable ones of this earth. (T&C 138:18-19)

Accordingly, there is always going to be a temple when the Holy Order is present in its fullest manifestation. Abraham also is directly associated with temple ritual. As Nibley explained, "There is a wealth of tradition now being zealously studied to show that the temple ordinances really go back to the beginning, as Joseph Smith declared. The four names associated with the tradition are those of Adam, Enoch, Abraham, and Elijah."[217]

To return a complete Restoration, a temple will be required. As the Lord revealed to Joseph, a temple is always required of God's people:

> For your oracles in your most holy places wherein you receive conversations, and your statutes and judgments for the beginning of the revelations and foundation of Zion, and for the glory, and honor, and endowment of all her municipals, are ordained by the ordinance of my holy house, which my people are always commanded to build unto my holy name. (T&C 141:12 [D&C 124:39])

The required temple in Nauvoo was **not** built. The fullness was not restored during Joseph Smith's lifetime. Instead of blessings, the

---

[217] *Temple and Cosmos*, Deseret Book 1992, p. 78.

saints were cursed.[218] Not only did the January 1841 revelation warn of cursing—including forcible expulsion from Nauvoo—but 22 months following that revelation (in an editorial on October 1, 1842), Joseph Smith pled for renewed focus on the temple. He wrote:

> Perhaps we have said enough on this subject, but we feel the importance of it and therefore speak plainly. It is for you, brethren, to say whether the work shall stand or progress; one thing is certain, that unless that is done all our efforts to aggrandize or enrich ourselves will be vain and futile. We may build splendid houses but we shall not inhabit them; we may cultivate farms but we shall not enjoy them; we may plant orchards, or vineyards, but we shall not eat the fruit of them. The word of the Lord is build my house, and until that command is fulfilled we stand responsible to the great Jehovah for the fulfilment of it, and if not done in due time we may have to share the same fate that we have heretofore done in Missouri.[219]

Joseph's warning did not inspire the saints. Their neglect and disobedience changed the warning into prophecy. They suffered the same fate as before in Missouri, even though the Lord wanted (and expected) better of them. There is no reason to repeat their failure, because the Lord does not reward the disobedient. He offers blessings, and it is up to His people to receive them through obedience. But if His offer is rejected, there are no secured promises.

In the "Answer to Prayer for Covenant," the Lord assures us that if we are faithful, we will be given[220] His temple:

> *I will visit my house, which the remnant of my people shall build, and I will dwell therein, to be among you, and no one will need to say, Know ye the Lord, for you all shall know me, from the least to the greatest. I will teach you things that have been hidden from the*

---

[218] The Lord warned in January 1841 that if the saints "do not do the things that I say, I will not perform the oath which I make unto you, neither fulfill the promises which you expect at my hands, says the Lord. For instead of blessings, you, by your own works, bring cursings, wrath, indignation, and judgments upon your own heads, by your follies and by all your abominations which you practice before me, says the Lord" (T&C 141:14 [D&C 124:47-48]).

[219] *JSP, Documents, Volume 11*, p. 127.

[220] Although we are required to build it, it will nevertheless be God's gift. He must authorize it. He must instruct and empower what takes place within it.

foundation of the world and your understanding will reach unto Heaven. (T&C 158:15-16)

The first and most complete religion belonged to Adam and Eve. They lived with God, and after being cast out, they retained a memory of living in God's presence.[221] The first Fathers were taught they could talk with God, receive answers from Him, and return to His presence. The experience of Enoch—seven generations after Adam—records that direct contact between mankind and God was part of the true religion. After the fall of mankind, the process of the ascent of man into Heaven to commune with God has remained the heart of the religion.[222] That process will reverse, and contact between mankind and God at the end will involve the descent of God from Heaven to visit His tabernacle:

*And Enoch beheld the Son of Man ascend up unto the Father, and he called unto the Lord, saying, Will you not come again upon the earth? For inasmuch as you are God, and I know you, and you have sworn unto me and commanded me that I should ask in the name of your Only Begotten, you have made me, and given unto me a right to your throne, and not of myself, but through your own grace. Wherefore, I ask you if you will not come again on the earth. And the Lord said unto Enoch, As I live, even so **will** I come in the last days, in the days of wickedness and vengeance, to fulfill the oath which I have made unto you concerning the children of Noah. And the day shall come that the earth shall rest. But before that day, the heavens shall be darkened, and a veil of darkness shall cover the earth; and the heavens shall shake, and also the earth. And great tribulations shall be among the children of men, but **my people will I preserve**. And **righteousness** will I send down out of Heaven. **Truth** will I send forth out of the earth to bear testimony of my Only Begotten, his resurrection from the dead, yea, and also the resurrection of all men. And righteousness and truth will I cause to sweep the earth as with a flood, to gather out my own elect from the four quarters of the earth unto a place which I shall prepare, a holy city, that my people may gird up their loins and be looking forth for the time of my coming. For there shall be my tabernacle, and it shall be called Zion, a New Jerusalem. And the Lord said unto Enoch, Then shall you and all your city meet them there,*

---

[221] See Lectures on Faith 2:36.
[222] See, e.g., Acts 4:10 [7:54-8:1]; Revelation 1:5 [1:12-16]; 1 Nephi 1:3 [1:5-15]; 3:9-14 [11:19-36]; 2 Nephi 8:2 [11:2-7]; Alma 17:5 [36:21-24]; Ether 1:12-14 [3:6-20]; JSH 2:4 [1:15-18]; T&C 69:5 [76:22-24]; 160:1; and 161:1-23, among others.

and we will receive them into our bosom. And they shall see us, and we will fall upon their necks, and they shall fall upon our necks, and we will kiss each other; and there shall be my abode. (Genesis 4:22 [Moses 7:58-63])

So that there are no false assumptions,[223] the Scriptures explain that God's covenant with Enoch includes an **actual** temple to be built today. And the Lord has reiterated in His Covenant: *I will come to my tabernacle and dwell with my people in Zion, and none will overtake it* (T&C 157:64, emphasis added).

The religion of the Fathers involved direct communion, contact, and connection between mankind and God. The Holy Order is an important part of the return of that direct association. The original religion of the Patriarchs enabled the faithful to hear directly from the Lord His promise of eternal life.[224] God would seal them by covenant into His Heavenly Family. We can, if faithful, obtain all that the original Fathers received from God at the beginning:

> *What I, the Lord, have spoken, I have spoken, and I excuse not myself. And though the heaven and the earth pass away, my word shall not pass away, but shall all be fulfilled, whether by my own voice or by the voice of my servants it is the same. For behold and lo, the Lord is God and the spirit bears record, and the record is true, and the truth abides for ever and ever. Amen.* (T&C 54:7 [D&C 1:38-39])

As a servant of God, I say with His authority that these promises are true, and He intends to fulfill them for His covenant people Israel. In the beginning, mankind was placed in a family. The first commandment to Father Adam and Mother Eve was to multiply and replenish the Earth.[225] The first man and woman were married. Their union produced the family of mankind. Every soul born into this Creation came from parents, and all were intended to be in a family.

The plan of salvation is covenantal and familial. The government of God is a family. If a family is established by covenant with God, it will be the only order that can survive death. In a very real sense, the

---

[223] The temple will be built by man, and it will be an actual building, not a metaphorical thing existing only in the heart of believers.
[224] See T&C 99:14-17.
[225] See Genesis 2:9 [Moses 2:28-31].

salvation of mankind now comes only through the family of Abraham. The God of Abraham and of Isaac and of Jacob covenanted with these three successive generations that they would stand at the head of all who would be saved after them. The God of Israel requires some part of mankind–however small–to be sealed into that line or be utterly wasted at His coming.

God has explained in Scripture how He intends to identify covenant Israel in the last days. After the death of King Solomon, Israel divided into two kingdoms:

- The first was the Northern Kingdom. After the division, these were sometimes called "Ephraim" or the "Ten Tribes" or "Israel" (in the Old Covenants).

- The second was the Southern Kingdom, called "Judah" (and later, "the Jews").[226]

The Northern Kingdom was conquered, taken captive, and removed from their land by Assyria in 722 BC.[227] When freed by Assyria years later, they crossed the Euphrates River and disappeared from our records into a far land.[228] They were only lost to our limited record of history.

The Southern Kingdom was conquered in 598 BC by Babylon, taken captive, and removed from their land. When Cyrus allowed their return in 538 BC,[229] only a remnant returned.[230]

Because of these two great exiles, the Ten Tribes were scattered and lost to our history, and the returning Jews were reduced to a small remnant of the original population. Today's Jews descended from that small remnant. The greater part of Israelite blood is in the Middle East. These descendants of the exiled Israelites remained, intermarried, and today are among the ancestors of Iranians, Iraqis,

---

[226] See 1 Kings 3:1-7 [12:1-20] for the division of Israel.

[227] "In the ninth year of Hoshea, the king of Assyria took Samaria and carried Israel away into Assyria, and placed them in Halah, and in Habor by the river of Gozan, and in the cities of the Medes" (2 Kings 5:18 [17:1-6]).

[228] See II Esdras 13:40-45 where their decision to go to an uninhabited location is recounted.

[229] See 2 Chronicles 19:9 [36:22-23]; Ezra 1:1-2 [1:1-11].

[230] "The whole congregation together was forty-two thousand three hundred sixty, besides their servants and their maids, of whom there were seven thousand three hundred thirty-seven" (Ezra 1:13 [2:64-65]).

Syrians, Turks, Jordanians, and Arabians. Israelites were also scattered into northern Europe and Asia among Europeans, Russians, and Scandinavians. As God promised to Abraham: Over the centuries, intermarriage and migration has sent his Israelite descendants into "all nations."[231] Today, almost all Israelite blood runs through the veins of people regarded as Gentiles because, after being scattered, they assimilated and lost their original identity.

Today's Jews are only a tiny fraction of the original Israelites. Their history has been marked by continual persecution. Their perseverance has been heroic. They are people of destiny and prophecy. However, many of the prophecies concerning Israel **do not involve the Jews.** In addition, Jews do not know the record of the Nephites. They have not been taught the prophecies of Joseph Smith. They are unaware of the covenant God renewed in 2017. Accordingly, many prophecies are unknown to and will not be fulfilled through the Jews.

It will only be through Israel that we can be sealed by a covenant with God to Heavenly Parents through the Fathers. Salvation is still through Israel. The question is: Where are we to find the prophesied last-days' Israel now?

The Book of Mormon relates how religious identities are changed by God. Jacob, the brother of Nephi, prophesied that *the gentiles shall be blessed and numbered among the house of Israel* (2 Nephi 7:4 [10:18]). His brother prophesied: *As many of the gentiles as will repent* **are** *the covenant people of the Lord* (2 Nephi 12:11 [30:2], emphasis added). Therefore, God promised to number Gentiles as people of Israel **by covenant.** That promise was realized in 2017 when He ordained a covenant for the Gentiles to re-establish them as His people.[232]

The Jews are still a remnant of covenant people. However, they can forfeit their status if they reject the covenant offered by the Lord in 2017: *As many of the Jews as will not repent shall be cast off. For the Lord covenanteth with none save it be with them that repent and believe in his Son, who is the Holy One of Israel* (ibid.).

---

[231] "I give unto you a promise that this right shall continue in you and in your seed after you (that is to say, the literal seed or the seed of the body) – shall all the families of the earth be blessed, even with the blessings of the gospel, which are the blessings of salvation, even of life eternal" (Abraham 3:1 [2:11]).

[232] See T&C 156, 157, and 158.

How we respond to God affects our covenant status.[233] When the resurrected Messiah visited the branch of Israel in the Americas, He quoted His Father about future covenantal realignment of identities. Covenant-status is now based on how individuals respond to the Holy One of Israel. *But if the gentiles will repent and return unto me, saith the **Father**, behold, they shall be numbered among my people, O house of Israel* (3 Nephi 7:5 [16:13], emphasis added).

The Messiah explained the process for a Gentile to change their identity:

> *The gentiles, if they will not harden their hearts, that they may repent, and come unto me, and be baptized in my name, and know of the true points of my doctrine, **that they may be numbered among my people, O house of Israel** – and when these things come to pass, that thy seed shall begin to know these things, it shall be a sign unto them that they may know that the work of the Father hath already commenced unto the fulfilling of the covenant which he hath made unto the people who are of the house of Israel.* (3 Nephi 9:11 [21:6-7], emphasis added)

> *But if [the gentiles] will repent, and hearken unto my words, and harden not their hearts, I will establish my church among them, and they shall come in unto the covenant and be numbered among this the remnant of Jacob, unto whom I have given this land for their inheritance. And they shall assist my people, the remnant of Jacob, and also as many of the house of Israel as shall come, that they may build a city which shall be called the New Jerusalem. And then shall they assist my people, that they may be gathered in, who are scattered upon all the face of the land, in unto the New Jerusalem. And then shall the Powers of Heaven come down among them, and I also will be in the midst.* (3 Nephi 10:1 [21:22-25])

---

[233] See, e.g., Alma 15:9 [27:25-30], where former rebellious Lamanites converted and were numbered among the people of Nephi, inheriting all the associated covenant blessings, as well as Alma 21:2 [45:2-14], declaring that when the Nephites completed their apostasy, they would become "extinct" as a people. Their extinction was because all remaining descendants would lose covenantal status and identity and then be numbered with the Lamanites. Helaman 2:4 [3:13-16] is to the same effect, affirming Nephites would be "no more called the Nephites, becoming wicked, and wild, and ferocious, yea, even becoming Lamanites." It flowed both ways, though, because later in 3 Nephi 1:11 [2:13-16], Lamanites converted and "those Lamanites who had united with the Nephites were numbered among the Nephites, and their curse was taken from them."

The Messiah quoted a prophecy from Isaiah to confirm it was always God's plan to change Gentiles into Israelites:

> *And then shall that which is written come to pass: Sing, O barren, thou that didst not bear; break forth into singing and cry aloud, thou that didst not travail with child;* **for more are the children of the desolate than the children of the married wife** [children of the desolate are the Gentiles; the married wife was Israel], *saith the Lord. Enlarge the place of thy tent and let them stretch forth the curtains of thy habitations; spare not, lengthen thy cords and strengthen thy stakes, for thou shalt break forth on the right hand and on the left, and thy* **seed shall inherit the gentiles** *and make the desolate cities to be inhabited.* (ibid., vs. 2 [22:1-3], quoting from Isaiah 19:4 [54:1-10], emphasis added)

As Moroni finished his father's abridged record, he added his own prophecy of the last-days' New Jerusalem to be built on the American continent. The occupants of that holy city are described in his prophecy: *And then cometh the New Jerusalem; and blessed are they who dwell therein, for it is they whose garments are white through the blood of the Lamb;* **and they are they who are numbered among the remnant of the seed of Joseph,** *who were of the house of Israel* (Ether 6:3 [13:10], emphasis added).

"Numbered among." Numbered among means covenantal status as the seed or descendants of Joseph.

The New Jerusalem will be built by covenant Israel. The group whom the Lord regards as His Israel is covenant-dependent. But a covenant must be kept.

There are two identifiable remnants of previous covenant people. One group is Native Americans who descend biologically from the Israelite-Nephite covenant people. The other is the Jews. Both are biologically connected to Israel, but they will be "cast off" if they reject the covenant now offered by God. And Gentiles may or may not be biologically connected to Israel but are **numbered** with Israel if they accept the covenant.

The New Jerusalem is to be built by a remnant of Israel, or to be more precise, it will be built by a remnant the Lord regards as covenant Israel. The Lord's "Answer to the Prayer for Covenant" accepted a body of believing Gentiles as His people of Israel. God's promises and prophecies about Israel in the last days began to be fulfilled in 2017 when the covenant He offered was accepted. The Lord said to those people:

> ***I will number you*** *among the remnant of Jacob, no longer outcasts, and **you** will inherit the promises of Israel.* ***You*** *shall be my people and* ***I*** *will be your God, and the sword will not devour you. And unto those who will receive will more be given, until they know the mysteries of God in full.*[234] *. . .I have redeemed you from being orphaned and taken you that you are no longer a widowed people.* (T&C 157:48,50, emphasis added)

The Gentiles who accepted the Lord's Covenant have been promised they:

> *...are now numbered with my people who are of the house of Israel...*[235]

God's "Answer" goes on to assure covenant Israel:

> *And I, the Lord your God, will be with you and will never forsake you, and I will lead you in the path which will bring peace to you in the troubling season now fast approaching.*
>
> *I will raise you up and protect you, abide with you, and gather you in due time, and this shall be a land of promise to you as your inheritance from me.*
>
> *The earth will yield its increase, and you will flourish upon the mountains and upon the hills, and the wicked will not come against you because the fear of the Lord will be with you.*
>
> *I will visit my house, which the remnant of my people shall build, and I will dwell therein, to be among you, and no one will need to say, Know ye the Lord, for you* ***all*** *shall know me, from the least to the greatest.*
>
> *I will teach you things that have been hidden from the foundation of the world and your understanding will reach unto Heaven.*

---

[234] Conditioned upon obeying the terms of His covenant.
[235] Also conditioned upon obeying the terms of His covenant.

And you shall be called the children of the Most High God, and I will preserve you against the harvest.

*And the angels sent to harvest the world will gather the wicked into bundles to be burned, but will **pass over you** as my peculiar treasure.* (T&C 158:10,12-18, emphasis added)

This refers to a second **literal** Passover.

The Lord's "strange act"[236] is approaching completion. The promises made to the Fathers are being vindicated. The Restoration has recommenced, and if we are faithful, it will not be paused or interrupted again. Although Israel's numbers are few, there have never been great numbers willing to sacrifice everything for God. One requirement for faith has always been the same: *A religion that does not require the sacrifice of all things never has power sufficient to produce the faith necessary unto life and salvation* (Lectures on Faith 6:7). The Lord said this about our day: *I tell you that [I] will come, and when [I do] come, [I] will avenge [my] saints speedily. Nevertheless, when the Son of Man comes, shall [I] find faith on the earth?* (Luke 10:6 [18:8]).

There are two groups God has (or will) covenant to preserve against the coming harvest.

- The first are those who made and keep the covenant the Lord offered in 2017. It changed all those who accepted it into covenant Israel. They have the right to inherit this land and will be preserved. As stated in the "Answer to [the] Prayer for Covenant": *And the angels sent to harvest the world will gather the wicked into bundles to be burned, but will pass over you as my peculiar treasure* (T&C 158:18).

- The second are those who will become part of the Holy Order and receive and practice the religion of the Fathers. God alone will decide how many and who will be invited into that order. We have no control over it. We have no right to decide who is worthy or unworthy to receive it. It is entirely the Lord's choice because we are rarely able to determine other people's hearts. The Lord told Joseph Smith bluntly that he was unable to tell

---

[236] See Isaiah 8:4 [28:14-22]; T&C 101:20 [D&C 101:92-95].

the righteous from the wicked.[237] We are in no better position than was Joseph. Therefore, we should leave it with the Lord to determine whether or not to invite men and women and, if so, who and how many. The Holy Order is as much—or more—a burden as a blessing.

As Hyrum Smith explained, God imposes restrictions:

> *For the mysteries of God are not given to all men; and unto those to whom they are given they are placed under restrictions to impart only such as God will command them, and the residue is to be kept in a faithful breast, otherwise he will be brought under condemnation. By this God will prove his faithful servants, who will be called and numbered with the chosen.* (T&C 152:2)

The Egyptian imitation of the Patriarchal religion kept hidden the most important parts of their religion away from public disclosure.[238] Hugh Nibley explained:

> Bleeker duly notes that "certain parts of temples were inaccessible to ordinary people" and that "the Egyptian temple was not meant to let the masses of the people participate in the religious services."[239]

This was because:

> The rites, "revealed to men by Osiris, the first mortal to be resurrected," were nothing less than the "Great Secret" of how mortals may become gods, taught in the temple "the place of the great secret."[240]

---

[237] "I do not say that you shall not show it unto the righteous; but as you cannot always judge the righteous, or as you cannot always tell the wicked from the righteous; therefore, I say unto you, hold your peace until I shall see fit to make all things known unto the world concerning the matter" (JSH 10:14 [D&C 10:36-37]).

[238] Egypt's ceremonial rites preserved a great body of teaching about events prior to and during the Creation, the world of the dead, and afterlife beyond the grave. But Egypt retained these as memories from the patriarchal era, not as a continuing, living experience. Abraham, like many other Hebrew prophets, ascended and experienced the same theophany and witnessed the same pre-Earth events, Creation, and future destiny of mankind as the first patriarchs. Egypt's ceremonies were not the equivalent for God's presence that Abraham experienced.

[239] Nibley, *The Message of the Joseph Smith Papyrii*, Deseret Book 1975, p. 86, citing CJ Bleeker, *Initiation, Studies in the History of Religion*, 1965, pp. 50-51.

[240] Ibid., p. 88, citing A Moret, Royante, pp. 147-149.

Margaret Barker explained the Christian tradition of restricting information available **even to the faithful**. She likened the early Christian practice of concealing some truths from believers by referring to Origen's *Homily 5 on Numbers*, explaining:

> ...the secrets of the temple which were guarded by the priests. Commenting on Numbers 4, the instructions for transporting the tabernacle through the desert, he emphasized that the family of Kohath were only permitted to carry the sacred objects but were not permitted to see what was in the holy place; then they had to cover the sacred objects with veils before handling them to others, who were only permitted to carry them. The mysteries of the Church were similar....[241]

Clement of Rome recorded that Peter quoted an unwritten teaching of Christ that admonished: "Keep the mysteries/secrets for me and the sons of my house."[242] The resurrected Messiah taught His closest peers things that were not told to other believers.[243]

Knowing God's plans does not always produce immediate joy.[244] Solomon made this comment after a life of learning: *In much wisdom is much grief; and he that increases knowledge increases sorrow* (Ecclesiastes 1:3 [1:18]). We should not be surprised to learn that initiation into God's mysteries can be troubling, disquieting, and even a burden.

If asked to carry a burden by God, do it willingly. If not asked, do not envy. Remember Alma's statement: *Behold, I am a man, and do sin in my*

---

[241] Margaret Barker, *The Great High Priest*, T&C Clark, London 2003, pp. 76-77.
[242] *Clementine Homilies* 19:20.
[243] "Origen, writing for the next generation, knew of an unwritten tradition which had been handed down from the time of the prophets. 'Jesus, who was greater than all these, conversed with his disciples in private, and especially in their secret retreats concerning the gospel of God, but the words which he uttered have not been preserved because it appeared to the evangelists that they could not be adequately conveyed to the multitude in writing or speech.' Jesus, he said, 'beheld these weighty secrets and made them known to a few.' There had been 'doctrines spoken in private to his genuine disciples" (ibid., p. 226).
[244] Isaiah was distressed: "Then said I, Woe is me, for I am undone because I am a man of unclean lips, and I dwell in the midst of a people of unclean lips; for my eyes have seen the King, the Lord of Hosts" (Isaiah 2:2 [6:5]). Lehi was overcome when he "saw and heard much. And because of the things which he saw and heard, he did quake and tremble exceedingly" (1 Nephi 1:3 [1:6]). Enoch was bitter at what he was shown: "And as Enoch saw thus, he had bitterness of soul, and wept over his brethren, and said unto the Heavens, I will refuse to be comforted" (Genesis 4:19 [Moses 7:44]).

wish, for I ought to be content with the things which the Lord hath allotted unto me (Alma 15:12 [29:3]). It is our common enemy who stirs up jealousy and envy rather than patience and meekness. Great works of God fail because mankind will not wait on the Lord.[245]

> *Behold, there are many called, but few are chosen, and why are they not chosen? Because their hearts are set so much upon the things of this world, and aspire to the honors of men, that they do not learn this one lesson – that the rights of the Priesthood are inseparably connected with the Powers of Heaven and that the Powers of Heaven cannot be controlled nor handled, only upon the principles of righteousness. That they may be conferred upon us, it is true, but when we undertake to cover our sins or to gratify our pride, our vain ambition, or to exercise control, or dominion, or compulsion, upon the souls of the children of men in **any** degree of unrighteousness, behold, the Heavens withdraw themselves, the spirit of the Lord is grieved, and when it is withdrawn, Amen to the priesthood or the authority of that man.* (T&C 139:5 [D&C 121:34-37], emphasis added)

The more God gives, the greater the peril. Weaknesses of appetites, ambitions, passions, and covetousness is akin to trying to navigate through a narrow pass, guarded by a great beast, pitiless and cruel, that destroys all those whose zeal and impatience brings them into the reach of the beast.[246] God has provided to us guidance on how to reach Zion. It requires self-discipline and meekness to follow the Lord rather than racing ahead of Him to destruction.

Our first Fathers experienced visions, ascended into Heaven, obtained promises of exaltation, and were transformed by their experiences **from men into angels of God**.[247] Joseph Smith attempted to bring this back as part of the Restoration. Margaret Barker has written about the use of the term "angel" anciently to

---

[245] See T&C 163:1-3.

[246] See T&C 163, *supra*.

[247] Angels have the role of teaching. They fulfill their duty by "shewing themselves unto them of strong faith and a firm mind in every form of godliness. And the office of their ministry is to call men unto repentance, and to fulfill and to do the work of the covenants of the Father which he hath made unto the children of men, to prepare the way among the children of men by declaring the word of Christ unto the chosen vessels of the Lord, that they may bear testimony of him; and by so doing, the Lord God prepareth the way that the residue of men may have faith in Christ" (Moroni 7:6 [7:30-32]). Those of a firm mind to whom they appear bring the same message and discharge the same angelic assignment and, therefore, have been regarded as angels themselves.

identify those who had encountered God's presence.[248] She also explains a Dead Sea Scroll text foretelling a return of that religion: "The Qumran Melchizedek text has a possible reading about people in the last days whose teachers have been kept hidden and secret; perhaps they have been preserving the older ways."[249] The return of that religion will more likely be through a last-days' restoration rather than through preservation.[250] But she is correct to anticipate its return.

The Book of Mormon has account after account of prophets receiving an audience with God the Father and His Only Begotten Son.[251] This is the older, heavenly ascent religion that began with Adam in the Garden.

Joseph was called to become a minister of salvation when he saw the heavens open.[252] He taught the idea of direct association with Christ as the promised Second Comforter during a visit to Ramus, Illinois on April 2, 1843. After quoting Christ's promises to not leave His followers comfortless because He and His Father would come to them and take up their abode with them,[253] Joseph explained, "Now what is this other Comforter? It is no more nor less than the Lord Jesus Christ himself.... When any man obtains this last Comforter he will have the personage of Jesus Christ to attend him or appear unto him from time to time."[254] *The appearing of the Father and the Son, in that verse,* **is** *a personal appearance; and the idea that the Father and the Son dwell in a man's heart is an old sectarian notion,* **and is false** (D&C 130:3,

---

[248] See *The Great Angel, A Study of Israel's Second God*, Westminster John Knox Press 1992, pp. 120-121.

[249] *The Great High Priest*, supra, p. 79.

[250] The November 1831 prophecy may well refer to both, "And they shall bring forth their rich treasures unto the children of Ephraim, my servants, and the boundaries of the everlasting hills shall tremble at their presence, and there shall they fall down and be crowned with glory, even in Zion, by the hands of the servants of the Lord, even the children of Ephraim" (T&C 58:3 [D&C 133:30-32])–the "rich treasures" being a preservation of texts kept hidden, and the "crown[ing]...by the hands of the servants of the Lord, even the children of Ephraim" being the restoration of ordinances, authority, and a temple.

[251] See, e.g., 1 Nephi 1:3 [1:5-15]; 3:9-14 [11:19-36]; 2 Nephi 8:2 [11:2-7]; Alma 17:5 [36:21-24]; and Ether 1:12-14 [3:6-20], among others.

[252] See JSH 3:3 [1:33-35].

[253] "If a man love me, he will keep my words, and my Father will love him, and we will come unto him and make our abode with him" (John 9:8 [14:23]).

[254] *TPJS*, pp. 150–151; *Words of Joseph Smith*, p. 5. See also John 9:8 [14:23].

emphasis added).²⁵⁵ This appearing of the Father and Son began with Adam²⁵⁶ and was intended to continue **in every** generation.

Although the teaching of Christ as the Second Comforter was taught by Joseph Smith and believed by LDS Mormons, it is now one of the teachings that has dwindled from LDS teaching. In a Boise LDS meeting, church apostle Dallin Oaks denounced the teaching of mortals needing to see the Lord as "a tactic of the adversary."²⁵⁷ Following that, the LDS Church removed a footnote from their King James Version John 14:16 which previously referred to Jesus Christ and replaced it with a reference to the "Holy Ghost."²⁵⁸ At the time I wrote the book, *The Second Comforter: Conversing with the Lord Through the Veil* (in 2006), the text explained orthodox LDS belief. Since then, however, that sect has abandoned the teaching. If that book were written today by a faithful member of that church, it would have to be revised to reflect the church's changed view. By leaving the text unchanged, it provides a current example of continuing dwindling in unbelief. Changing belief into unbelief happens **very** quickly. *The Second Comforter: Conversing with the Lord Through the Veil* was published in 2006, and the doctrine was denounced as a "tactic of the adversary" by an LDS apostle in an official church meeting in 2015– only nine years later.

Joseph Smith's mission was to recover and restore. He may have seemed every bit an innovator and revolutionary, but the truth is that he was the **greatest religious reactionary**²⁵⁹ since Jesus Christ. The recovery through Joseph ended with his and Hyrum's murder,

---

255 Section 130 of the LDS Doctrine and Covenants first appeared as canon in the 1876 edition prepared by Orson Pratt under the direction of Brigham Young. It is used here for reference. For original sources, see *JSP, Journals, Volume 2*, pp. 323–326, 2 April 1843. Willard Richards didn't accompany Joseph Smith on his four-day trip to Ramus, IL, and he reconstructed the Joseph Smith Journal entry from the Journal of William Clayton (see *JSP, Journals, Volume 2*, pp. 403–405, Appendix 2, 1–4 April 1843; *Words of Joseph Smith*, p. 169, p. 267n3, p. 268n14).

256 See T&C 154:19 [D&C 107:53-55].

257 As part of the meeting, the following question and answer was covered: "Another claim is that the Church is not teaching what is necessary for exaltation. For example, some say that only those who see the face of Jesus Christ in mortality will receive Celestial Glory." Dallin H. Oaks: "Of course, all of the righteous desire to see the face of our Savior, but the suggestion that this must happen in mortality is a familiar tactic of the adversary." This event was recorded and can be viewed on YouTube (see "Boise Rescue," June 13, 2015, www.youtube.com).

258 The John 14:16 KJV footnote in the LDS Scriptures used to reference: "TG Jesus Christ, Second Comforter." That was changed and now reads: "TG Holy Ghost, Comforter."(The reference to "TG" is to the Topical Guide in the LDS publication.)

259 A reactionary seeks to restore a past tradition believed to be more correct and enlightened than the current status quo.

after which dwindling began. Dwindling in unbelief continued until a group repented and the Lord removed His condemnation in 2017. Now we hope to continue faithful. Christ commanded in the Sermon on the Mount: *Wherefore, seek not the things of this world, but seek first to build up the kingdom of God and to establish his righteousness, and all these things shall be added unto you* (Matthew 3:39 [6:33]).

There is a chapter in Hugh Nibley's book, *Temple and Cosmos*, titled "One Eternal Round: The Hermetic Tradition." That chapter goes from page 379 through 433, and it is worth reading in its entirety. However, I am going to lift a few quotes from his explanation of history that should seem familiar:

> In each dispensation the world went bad while the prophets united in futile protest, as in the days of Samuel, Hezekiah, Isaiah, and Jeremiah. In the powerful phrase of Ether, "the prophets mourned and withdrew from among the people."

> ...When not preaching it was their custom to keep a low profile, or simply to depart from the scene in the time-honored manner of the Rechabites, a pattern we find repeated over and over again in the Book of Mormon and vividly depicted in the Dead Sea Scrolls. The holy outcasts would form with their followers a community of saints, a church, waiting and working for Zion. Zion itself is a model of such a retreat from the world: "And from thence went forth the saying, ZION IS FLED." In their retreat the righteous refugees take particular pains to preserve the sacred records—we think of Moses, of John, of Ether, of Moroni, etc., preserving studying, and editing the sacred writings by special command.

> ...the esoteric community was limited to those who understood and could be trusted with the deeper meaning of the doctrine.

> ...Throughout the Book of Mormon the church itself regularly splits into a worldly society, notably the religion of the Nehors, and others consisting of "a few...humble followers of Christ" to whom special gifts and revelations were given.

...The gospel that the retreating wise men take with them into hiding is guarded as a secret, and that by express command. Why seek it? The jealousy and envy of others can be dangerous; they resent being shut out from something great and mysterious, like boys excluded from the club tree house. They usually take out their wrath and frustration by wrecking the place.

...[True worshipers] are naturally drawn to each other and excite ever-mounting distrust, suspicion, and envy of those excluded from the magic circle. "I was destined to prove a disturber and an annoyer of his (Satan's) kingdom," said Joseph Smith. ...We all know how the public received the prophet Joseph, who was placed in the greatest danger, not from angry outsiders, but from his jealous followers, like the Higbees and the Laws. The ancient Ephesians passed a law banishing great achievers from the city—they were a standing rebuke to the rest: "If they must excel," they said, "let them go and excel over somebody else." ...Anything they don't understand makes dogs and people uncomfortable, distrusting, and dangerous.

...We may consider the gospel as the most advanced knowledge on earth, known to but a few because it is accepted and believed by but a few and can be understood by no others.

...In ancient times, apostasy never came by renouncing the gospel but always by corrupting it. No one renounces it today, and so we have the strange paradox of people stoutly proclaiming beliefs and ideas that they have no intention of putting into practice.

...We seek knowledge as our greatest treasure, while the poverty of most of our manuals and handbooks defies description.

...The great apostasy in the time of the apostles was not a renouncing of the faith but its corruption and manipulation.

...Everywhere we find myths and legends about how the primal bond that existed between heaven and earth in the Golden Age was broken by the wickedness of men; the great common assemblies ceased and the gods departed. But, as Aristotle notes, some bits of the old knowledge always survived to the next age. ...the three things in the mysteries that Herodotus would never talk about were (1) the grand mystery of the true nature and character of God, which could be known only by revelation, (2) the ordinances by which the mysteries were taught and implemented, and (3) the doctrine or rationale of the whole, including that which explained the rites.

...Philosophy is the road, not the goal, which it never reaches. If you want answers to the questions which it proposes, you can get them in the end only by revelation.

...Joseph Smith points this out: "As Paul said, 'the world by wisdom know(s) not God,' so the world by speculation (is) destitute of revelation." Religion answers by private but nonnegotiable spiritual experiences.

...[Isaac] Newton also talked as Joseph Smith did, that "truth had been given by God [at] the beginning, but had been fragmented and corrupted in the course of time; its traces survived in enigmatic form in these different sorts of literature, but had to be recovered by a sort of dialectic between hard, disciplined inquiry and the ancient sources."

...Joseph explained to the brethren the ordinances and covenants "on to the highest Melchizedek Priesthood, setting forth the order pertaining to the Ancient of Days, and all those plans and principles by which anyone is enabled to secure the fullness of those blessings which have been prepared for the church of the First Born, and come up and abide in the presence of the Eloheim in the eternal worlds. In this council was instituted the ancient Order of things for the first time in these last days." All these teachings are given "knowing assuredly that all these things referred to in this council are always governed by the principle of revelation." The cosmic aspect of these mysteries was not neglected for, as Joseph said, "The ancients ...were (not) so ignorant of the system of heaven as many suppose."[260]

---

[260] All references and footnotes from the chapter are omitted.

These few excerpts from Hugh Nibley illustrate the tension between sacred knowledge and dwindling in unbelief. Facsimile No. 2 in the Book of Abraham is an example of a hypocephalus. These first appeared in 400 BC, and most examples reckon from very late in the Ptolemaic era.[261] These documents were developed because **the priests realized that sacred knowledge was slipping away and needed to be preserved**. One recent study of the hypocephalus concluded these circular funerary documents were "a synthesis of the widespread theological knowledge of the priests."[262]

They were used in only a few burials. "It is clear that the use of the hypocephalus never became widespread. Hypocephali remained exclusive pieces of funerary equipment reserved for the clergy and for the members of their families who occupied priestly positions in the *pallacide* of the temples."[263]

The Facsimile No. 2 was produced **at the end of the dwindling Egyptian religion in its final stages**, still *seeking earnestly to imitate that order established by the fathers in the first generations, in the days of the first Patriarchal reign, even in the reign of Adam* (Abraham 2:3 [1:26]). That facsimile is both a powerful symbol of what the Restoration promised and how it has dwindled. The original hypocephalus was intended to preserve sacred, hidden knowledge for use by the faithful and initiated priestly inner-circle. But it was written at a moment when the priests realized their sacred knowledge was slipping away. They were only able to make a gesture to preserve it by sketching a montage of ancient hieroglyphs to echo their dwindling religion. That document aptly symbolizes Joseph's calling to restore the lost, original, sacred knowledge. But Joseph's efforts have also dwindled for nearly two centuries. The opportunity to recover and practice the original religion still exists if the conditions of God's covenant are met.

---

[261] Facsimile No. 2 could not reckon from the time of Abraham because hypocephali were first developed about 1700 years after his lifetime. Therefore, the facsimile is connected as part of the text only because it illustrates ancient Egyptian beliefs from as far back as Abraham's lifetime. Facsimile No. 2 touches on Abraham's life or experiences only indirectly in figures 3 and 7, both of which mention priesthood and key words Abraham received. Neither of these suggests Egyptians had or understood these things. Knowledge about these beliefs had slipped away at the time hypocephali were created, and the priests were trying to pass along some echo, however limited, for the mummy to make use of in his afterlife.

[262] Tamas Mekis, *The Hypocephalus: an Ancient Egyptian Funerary Amulet,* Archaeopress Oxford, England 2020, p. 75.

[263] Ibid., p. 2, italics in original.

God overthrew the Egyptian gods by sending Moses.²⁶⁴ God overthrew the kingdom of the Jews by sending John as forerunner for His Son, the Messiah.²⁶⁵ God overthrew the Christian gods by sending Joseph Smith.²⁶⁶ Last of all, God renewed and restored life to His people in 2017 when He made a new covenant.²⁶⁷ Every time God acts, He overthrows all other false faiths to reaffirm His own religion. God's goal is always to revive it in its fullness, but that has been rarely achieved.²⁶⁸ He is actively restoring again today. This work is His, and it will continue until reaching its fullness. I am a witness of His hand moving, His voice speaking, His will being revealed, and His guidance being provided continually as His work unfolds line upon line, precept upon precept.²⁶⁹ We will see it succeed if we have the faith and patience²⁷⁰ to allow it to do so.

"Each of the great dispensations of the gospel has come in a time of world upheaval, when the waywardness of the human race has been matched by a climactic restlessness of the elements."²⁷¹

The overthrow of Egypt's gods by signs and wonders has inspired people (from ancient Israel to modern writers) with thoughtful reflection.²⁷² When the signs and plagues are viewed from the Egyptian religious perspective (to the extent we have been able to

---

²⁶⁴ The signs, wonders, and plagues involved the four great guardians:
- Michael, who in mortality was Adam, is associated with air–"breath of life" (Genesis 2:11 [Moses 3:4-7]).
- Gabriel, who in mortality was Noah, is associated with water–"the flood" (Genesis 5:12 [Moses 8:28-30]).
- Raphael, who in mortality was Enoch, is associated with fire–the "fiery ascent" (Genesis 4:23 [Moses 7:65-69]), and
- Uriel, who in mortality was John the Beloved, is associated with land–who "tarries on earth" (TSJ 12:20 [John 21:23]).

These four angelic guardians controlled the elements that were turned against the Egyptians and directly challenged and defeated the false Egyptian gods, with the three days of darkness (see Exodus 7:4 [10:21-29]) defeating even Ra.

²⁶⁵ See T&C 82:14 [D&C 84:25-28].

²⁶⁶ The First Vision opened a new dispensation, and the Book of Mormon clarified Joseph's role as a restorer sent by God to renew the faith once delivered to the apostles by Christ.

²⁶⁷ See T&C 156, 157, and 158.

²⁶⁸ Adam, Enoch, Melchizedek, and the Nephites following Christ's resurrection are the notable examples entrusted with that fullness.

²⁶⁹ See Isaiah 8:3 [28:9-13]; see also T&C 151:17 [D&C 128:21].

²⁷⁰ The opponents are often inside the body of believers. Aspiring, jealous, lustful, envious, and contentious spirits of the believers in past dispensations have done as much or more harm to God's purposes than the active opposition of disbelievers.

²⁷¹ Nibley, *Abraham in Egypt*, supra, p. 164.

²⁷² From the *Aramaic Targum* of Exodus to Val Brinkerhoff's paper *God's 12 Signs in Egypt*, the account of the Egyptian plagues have inspired libraries of reflection. to

reconstruct that view), the God of Israel directly challenged the gods of Egypt.

The competing serpents described in Exodus 4:11 [7:8-13] was a direct conflict between the power of Israel's God and the Egyptian magicians. To Egypt, the serpent symbolized Apophis, the force of chaos. For Israelites, the brass serpent was to become a symbolic representation of their future Messiah. A serpent made of brass, raised up on a pole for suffering Israelites to look upon to be healed,[273] foreshadowed the atoning sacrifice of Jesus the Messiah.[274]

Moses' staff became a serpent that ate the Egyptian magicians' serpents. The incident demonstrated the Messiah's power to overthrow destruction and chaos. The event should have taught the Egyptian Pharaoh that Israel's God held all power.

The plagues that began with Egyptian water turning to blood was a direct defeat of the Nile god, Hapi. That first plague and the final destruction both involved authority over water. Gabriel poisoned the Nile at the beginning and completed the overthrow when the waters of the Red Sea returned to drown Pharaoh's horsemen and chariots.[275]

Pharaoh witnessed the defeat of other Egyptian gods. Hathor was overthrown when the Egyptian cattle died, while the Israelite cattle were spared.[276]

Geb was overthrown when dust under Uriel's stewardship was sent to afflict the Egyptian's skin with boils.[277]

Fire was sent by Raphael with burning hail and loud thunder.[278] Later, a pillar of smoke by day and fire by night unmistakably signified Raphael's protection for Israel.[279]

---

[273] See Numbers 10:7 [21:6-9].
[274] See John 8:3 [12:27-36].
[275] See Exodus 9:4 [14:21-31].
[276] See Exodus 6:1 [9:1-7].
[277] See Exodus 6:2 [9:8-12].
[278] See Exodus 6:5 [9:20-26].
[279] See Exodus 8:10 [13:20-22].

Michael sent the east wind and locusts to destroy the crops of Egypt.[280] Then Michael blocked the light of Ra,[281] overthrowing the Egyptian deity believed to have power over all Creation, including the underworld. Michael removed the breath of life from every firstborn in Egypt[282] that finally led to Egypt's surrender. The power of Israel's God and the combined acts of His archangels proved too much to resist.

Egypt believed there were "four sons of Horus." This idea was left over from the Patriarchal era and was their apostate belief that roughly corresponded to the four archangels: Michael, Gabriel, Raphael, and Uriel. Yet Egypt chose to fight against these four until they were destroyed. Once Egypt was defeated, for centuries Israel's religion increased, and Egypt's waned. Eventually, this led to the ultimate death of Egypt's religion. So complete was the God of Israel's overthrow of Egypt that the Egyptian language itself was altogether lost until the Rosetta Stone made it possible to reconstruct (in part) the identities of some of Egypt's defeated gods and fragments of Egypt's ancient beliefs.

In another conflict, John the Baptist was ordained by God's angel when eight days old to overthrow the kingdom of the Jews.[283] Joseph Smith explained John the Baptist "wrested the keys, the kingdoms, the power, the glory from the Jews, by the holy anointing and decree of heaven."[284] He went before the Messiah, as foretold by Gabriel to his father, Zechariah.[285] The Messiah's forerunner fulfilled Isaiah's prophecy[286] and testified to the Jews that Jesus was their Messiah. Once the Messiah had been lifted up, God destroyed the Jewish nation and demolished their temple.[287]

After nearly two millennia, Joseph Smith ended the Christian God's silence by declaring the heavens had opened and the Father and Son had appeared to and spoken with him.[288] In the following two decades, ancient Scripture from Adam, Enoch, Melchizedek,

---

[280] See Exodus 7:3 [10:12-20].
[281] See Exodus 7:4 [10:21-29].
[282] See Exodus 8:5 [12:29-36].
[283] See T&C 82:14 [D&C 84:25-28].
[284] *TPJS* p. 276, *WJS* p. 234, 236.
[285] See Luke 1:3-4 [1:8-25], also called Zacharias.
[286] See Isaiah 14:1 [40:3-8]; Luke 3:4 [3:4-6].
[287] See Josephus, *The Jewish War*, 6:4.
[288] See JSH 2:4-5 [1:15-20].

Abraham, and Moses was restored, the Bible corrected and expanded, new revelations and commandments provided, and lost authority to act in God's name was returned.

In 2014, God revoked the authority of the LDS hierarchy.[289] In the ensuing few years, that institution has continually stumbled into darkness and disarray, with their temples closed[290] and services altogether interrupted for a year. They have voluntarily altered and abandoned parts of their temple rites.[291] They have voluntarily chosen to destroy the original Salt Lake Temple[292] and replace it with a modern substitute lacking the original symbolism and meaning. They have continually surrendered to popular opinion and increasingly adopted the worldly agenda of accepting sexual confusion,[293] political intolerance,[294] and censorship of opinion. When viewed as trends, it becomes apparent the LDS Church's leadership is rapidly moving in a direction contrary to its original roots.[295]

In contrast, a small group has been repenting and returning to the original roots established by God through Joseph Smith.[296] By 2017,

---

[289] See T&C 166:2-3.

[290] March 25, 2020 letter of the First Presidency.

[291] Changes were made in January 2019. When introduced, it was accompanied with this explanation: "These adjustments, which you will notice during your worship experience in the temple today, will bring harmony to the way men and women make covenants with God. They deepen our understanding of His will and His relationship with his daughters and sons."

[292] See LDS *Church News*, 12 March 2021, "First Presidency announces Salt Lake Temple changes–increasing capacity, impacting live sessions; Manti temple next for renovation," in which the removal of pioneer murals and replacement of the live endowment with film is announced.

[293] See LDS *Church News*, 4 April 2019, "Policy Changes Announced for Members in Gay Marriages, Children of LGBT Parents" and also 2020 *LDS Handbook of Instructions*, characterized by the media as softening that church's stance on sexuality.

[294] White progressives using the term "Antifa" who seek the overthrow of the U.S. Government and its replacement with a communist dictatorship largely compose those who support the Marxist "Black Lives Matter" movement. Matthew Lohmeier addresses this at length in his upcoming book, *Irresistible Revolution: Marxism's Goal of Conquest & The Unmaking of the American Military*. The book is scheduled for release later this year. In contrast, Dallin Oaks of the LDS Twelve Apostles, in a speech at Brigham Young University, declared: "'Of course Black lives matter. That is an eternal truth all reasonable people should support,' said the first counselor in the First Presidency of The Church of Jesus Christ of Latter-day Saints" (*BYU Daily Universe*, October 27, 2020, "President Dallin H. Oaks says Black lives matter, urges all to rely on Christ during challenges").

[295] It is descending downward to destruction with other religions, as foretold in T&C 172.

[296] See T&C 156.

a more accurate version of the Book of Mormon was recovered, the JST Bible revisions were accurately published for the first time,[297] the Lectures on Faith returned to the canon,[298] additional Scriptures added, and a new covenant with God was established.[299]

Overthrowing and returning are repeated cycles, and they are underway again today. But the overthrow and the returning are not yet complete. The overthrow **will bring a full end to all nations**[300] **and religions,**[301] but the returning will be determined by covenant-keeping.

In the name of Jesus Christ, Amen.

---

[297] See "Preface" in the Old Covenants that explains the history of the JST and includes this: "This Restoration Edition of the Old Testament encompasses every change Joseph Smith made, whether they were in the version published by the RLDS Church or not; also, all of the editorial changes that were inserted by their committee have been eliminated."
[298] See T&C 110.
[299] See T&C 158.
[300] See T&C 85:3 [D&C 87:6-7].
[301] See T&C 172:5.

THE BOOK OF ABRAHAM

Translated through Joseph Smith primarily in November 1835, and published in the Times and Seasons 1 March–16 May 1842.

Facsimile 1

A FACSIMILE FROM THE BOOK OF ABRAHAM
NO. 1

Explanation of the above cut

Fig. 1. The angel of the Lord.
2. Abraham, fastened upon an altar.
3. The idolatrous priest of Elkkener attempting to offer up Abraham as a sacrifice.

4. The altar for sacrifice, by the idolatrous priests, standing before the gods of Elkkener, Zibnah, Mahmackrah, Koash, and Pharaoh.
5. The idolatrous god of Elkkener.
6. The "   "   "   Zibnah.
7. The "   "   "   Mahmackrah.
8. The "   "   "   Koash.
9. The "   "   "   Pharaoh.
10. Abraham in Egypt.
11. Designed to represent the Pillars of Heaven, as understood by the Egyptians.
12. Raukeeyang, signifying expanse, or the firmament over our heads; but in this case, in relation to this subject, the Egyptians meant it to signify shamau: to be high, or the heavens, answering to the Hebrew word, shaumahyeem.

Chapter 1

In the land of the Chaldeans, at the residence of my father, I, Abraham, saw that it was needful for me to obtain another place of residence. And finding there was greater happiness, and peace, and rest for me, I sought for the blessings of the Fathers and the right whereunto I should be ordained to administer the same. Having been myself a follower of righteousness, desiring also to be one who possessed great knowledge, and to be a greater follower of righteousness, and to possess a greater knowledge, and to be a Father of many nations, a prince of peace, and desiring to receive instructions and to keep the commandments of God, I became a rightful heir, a high priest, holding the right belonging to the Fathers. It was conferred upon me from the Fathers: it came down from the Fathers, from the beginning of time, yea, even from the beginning (or before the foundations of the earth) to the present time, even the right of the firstborn (or the first man – who is Adam – or first Father) through the Fathers unto me. I sought for my appointment unto the Priesthood according to the appointment of God unto the Fathers concerning the seed.

2 My fathers having turned from their righteousness, and from the holy commandments which the Lord, their God, had given unto them, unto the worshipping of the gods of the heathens, utterly refused to hearken to my voice. For their hearts were set to do evil, and were wholly turned to the god of Elkkener, and the god of Zibnah, and the god of Mahmackrah, and the god of Koash, and the god of Pharaoh, king of Egypt. Therefore, they turned their hearts to the sacrifice of the heathen in offering up their children unto their dumb idols, and hearkened not unto my voice, but endeavored to take away my life by the hand of the priest of Elkkener; the priest of Elkkener was also the priest of Pharaoh.

3 Now, at this time it was the custom of the priest of Pharaoh, the king of Egypt, to offer up upon the altar which was built in the land of Chaldea, for the offering unto these strange gods, both men, women, and children. And it came to pass that the priest made an offering unto the god of Pharaoh and also unto the god of Shagreel, even after the manner of the Egyptians. Now the god of Shagreel was the sun. Even the thank-offering of a child did the priest of Pharaoh offer upon the altar which stood by the hill called Potipher's Hill, at the head of the plain of Olishem. Now this priest had offered upon this altar three virgins at one time who were the

daughters of Onitah, one of the royal descent directly from the loins of Ham. These virgins were offered up because of their virtue – they would not bow down to worship gods of wood or of stone; therefore, they were killed upon this altar, and it was done after the manner of the Egyptians.

4 And it came to pass that the priests laid violence upon me that they might slay me also, as they did those virgins, upon this altar. And that you might have a knowledge of this altar, I will refer you to the representation at the commencement of this record. It was made after the form of a bedstead, such as was had among the Chaldeans, and it stood before the gods of Elkkener, Zibnah, Mahmackrah, Koash, and also a god like unto that of Pharaoh, king of Egypt. That you may have an understanding of these gods, I have given you the fashion of them in the figures at the beginning, which manner of the figures is called by the Chaldeans Kahleenos, which signifies hieroglyphics.

5 And as they lifted up their hands upon me that they might offer me up and take away my life, behold, I lifted up my voice unto the Lord, my God. And the Lord hearkened and heard, and he filled me with a vision of the Almighty. And the angel of his presence stood by me and immediately unloosed my bands, and his voice was unto me: Abram, Abram. Behold, my name is Jehovah, and I have heard you, and have come down to deliver you, and to take you away from your father's house and from all your kin-folks, into a strange land which you know not of, and this because they have turned their hearts away from me to worship the god of Elkkener, and the god of Zibnah, and the god of Mahmackrah, and the god of Koash, and the god of Pharaoh, king of Egypt. Therefore, I have come down to visit them and to destroy him who has lifted up his hand against you, Abram, my son, to take away your life. Behold, I will lead you by my hand, and I will take you, to put upon you my name, even the Priesthood of your Father, and my power shall be over you. As it was with Noah, so shall it be with you, that through your ministry my name shall be known in the earth for ever, for I am your God.

Chapter 2

Behold, Potipher's Hill was in the land of Ur of Chaldea, and the Lord broke down the altar of Elkkener, and of the gods of the land, and utterly destroyed them, and smote the priest that he died.

And there was great mourning in Chaldea, and also in the court of Pharaoh, which Pharaoh signifies king by royal blood.

2 Now this king of Egypt was a descendant from the loins of Ham and was a partaker of the blood of the Canaanites by birth. From this descent sprang all the Egyptians, and thus the blood of the Canaanites was preserved in the land, the land of Egypt being first discovered by a woman, who was the daughter of Ham and the daughter of Zeptah, which, in the Chaldea, signifies Egypt, which signifies that which is forbidden. When this woman discovered the land it was under water, who afterward settled her sons in it. And thus from Ham sprang that race which preserved the curse in the land.

3 Now the first government of Egypt was established by Pharaoh, the eldest son of Egyptes, the daughter of Ham, and it was after the manner of the government of Ham, which was Patriarchal. Pharaoh, being a righteous man, established his kingdom and judged his people wisely and justly all his days, seeking earnestly to imitate that order established by the fathers in the first generations, in the days of the first Patriarchal reign, even in the reign of Adam, and also Noah, his father, who blessed him with the blessings of the earth, and with the blessings of wisdom, but cursed him as pertaining to the Priesthood. Now Pharaoh being of that lineage by which he could not have the right of Priesthood, notwithstanding the Pharaohs would fain claim it from Noah through Ham, therefore my father was led away by their idolatry. But I shall endeavor hereafter to delineate the chronology running back from myself to the beginning of the creation, for the records have come into my hands, which I hold unto this present time.

4 Now after the priest of Elkkener was smitten that he died, there came a fulfillment of those things which were said unto me concerning the land of Chaldea, that there should be a famine in the land. Accordingly, a famine prevailed throughout all the land of Chaldea, and my father was sorely tormented because of the famine and he repented of the evil which he had determined against me – to take away my life. But the records of the Fathers, even the Patriarchs, concerning the right of Priesthood, the Lord, my God, preserved in my own hands. Therefore, a knowledge of the beginning of the creation, and also of the planets and of the stars, as they were made known unto the Fathers, have I kept even unto this

day, and I shall endeavor to write some of these things upon this record for the benefit of my posterity that shall come after me.

5 Now the Lord God caused the famine to wax sore in the land of Ur, insomuch that Haran, my brother, died, but Terah, my father, yet lived in the land of Ur of the Chaldees. And it came to pass that I, Abraham, took Sarai to wife, and Nahor, my brother, took Milcah to wife, who were the daughters of Haran. Now the Lord had said unto me, Abram, get yourself out of your country, and from your kindred, and from your father's house, unto a land that I will show you. Therefore, I left the land of Ur of the Chaldees, to go into the land of Canaan; and I took Lot, my brother's son, and his wife, and Sarai, my wife, and also my father followed after me, unto the land which we denominated Haran. And the famine abated; and my father tarried in Haran and dwelt there, as there were many flocks in Haran. And my father turned again unto his idolatry, therefore he continued in Haran.

Chapter 3

But I, Abram, and Lot, my brother's son, prayed unto the Lord, and the Lord appeared unto me and said unto me, Arise and take Lot with you, for I have purposed to take you away out of Haran, and to make of you a minister to bear my name in a strange land which I will give unto your seed after you for an everlasting possession, when they hearken to my voice, for I am the Lord, your God. I dwell in Heaven; the earth is my footstool. I stretch my hand over the sea and it obeys my voice; I cause the wind and the fire to be my chariot; I say to the mountains, Depart hence, and behold, they are taken away by a whirlwind, in an instant, suddenly. My name is Jehovah, and I know the end from the beginning. Therefore, my hand shall be over you, and I will make of you a great nation, and I will bless you above measure, and make your name great among all nations. And you shall be a blessing unto your seed after you, that in their hands they shall bear this ministry and Priesthood unto all nations. And I will bless them through your name; for as many as receive this gospel shall be called after your name and shall be accounted your seed, and shall rise up and bless you, as unto their Father. And I will bless them that bless you and curse them that curse you. And in you (that is, in your Priesthood) and in your seed, (that is, your Priesthood) – for I give unto you a promise that this right shall continue in you and in your seed after you (that is to say, the literal seed or the seed of the body) – shall all the families of the earth be blessed, even with the blessings of the gospel, which are the blessings of salvation, even of life eternal.

2 Now, after the Lord had withdrawn from speaking to me and withdrawn his face from me, I said in my heart, Your servant has sought you earnestly, now I have found you. You did send your angel to deliver me from the gods of Elkkener, and I will do well to hearken unto your voice; therefore, let your servant rise up and depart in peace.

Chapter 4

So I, Abram, departed as the Lord had said unto me, and Lot with me. And I, Abram, was sixty and two years old when I departed out of Haran. And I took Sarai, whom I took to wife when I was in Ur, in Chaldea, and Lot, my brother's son, and all our substance that we had gathered, and the souls that we had won in Haran, and came forth in the way to the land of Canaan, and dwelt in tents as we came on our way. Therefore, eternity was our covering, and our rock, and our salvation, as we journeyed from Haran by the way of Jershon, to come to the land of Canaan.

2 Now I, Abram, built an altar in the land of Jershon, and made an offering unto the Lord, and prayed that the famine might be turned away from my father's house, that they might not perish. And then we passed from Jershon through the land unto the place of Sechem. It was situated in the plains of Moreh, and we had already come into the borders of the land of the Canaanites. And I offered sacrifice there in the plains of Moreh and called on the Lord devoutly, because we had already come into the land of this idolatrous nation. And the Lord appeared unto me in answer to my prayers and said unto me, Unto your seed I will give this land. And I, Abraham, arose from the place of the altar which I had built unto the Lord, and removed from thence unto a mountain on the east of Beth-el and pitched my tent there: Beth-el on the west, and Hai on the east. And there I built another altar unto the Lord and called again upon the name of the Lord.

3 And I, Abraham, journeyed, going on still toward the south. And there was a continuation of a famine in the land, and I, Abraham, concluded to go down into Egypt, to sojourn there, for the famine became very grievous.

4 And it came to pass when I was come near to enter into Egypt, the Lord said unto me, Behold, Sarai, your wife, is a very fair woman to look upon; therefore, it shall come to pass when the Egyptians shall see her they will say, She is his wife, and they will kill you, but they will save her alive. Therefore, see that you do on this wise: let her say unto the Egyptians, she is your sister, and your soul shall live. And it came to pass that I, Abraham, told Sarai, my wife, all that the Lord had said unto me – therefore say unto them, I pray you, you are my sister, that it may be well with me for your sake, and my soul shall live because of you.

Chapter 5

And I, Abraham, had the Urim and Thummim which the Lord, my God, had given unto me in Ur of the Chaldees. And I saw the stars also, that they were very great, and that one of them was nearest unto the throne of God. And there were many great ones which were near unto it. And the Lord said unto me, These are the governing ones, and the name of the great one is Kolob because it is near unto me, for I am the Lord, your God; I have set this one to govern all those which belong to the same order of that upon which you stand. And the Lord said unto me by the Urim and Thummim that Kolob was after the manner of the Lord, according to its times and seasons in the revolutions thereof; that one revolution was a day unto the Lord after his manner of reckoning, it being one thousand years according to the time appointed unto that whereon you stand. This is the reckoning of the Lord's time according to the reckoning of Kolob.

2 And the Lord said unto me, The planet which is the lesser light, lesser than that which is to rule the day, even the night, is above or greater than that upon which you stand, in point of reckoning, for it moves in order more slow. This is in order because it stands above the earth upon which you stand; therefore, the reckoning of its time is not so many as to its number of days, and of months, and of years. And the Lord said unto me, Now, Abraham, these two facts exist; behold, your eyes see it. It is given unto you to know the times of reckoning and the set times. Yea, the set time of the earth upon which you stand, and the set time of the greater light which is set to rule the day, and the set time of the lesser light which is set to rule the night. Now the set time of the lesser light is a longer time as to its reckoning than the reckoning of the time of the earth upon

which you stand. And where these two facts exist, there shall be another fact above them. That is, there shall be another planet whose reckoning of time shall be longer still. And thus there shall be the reckoning of the time of one planet above another until you come nigh unto Kolob, which Kolob is after the reckoning of the Lord's time, which Kolob is set nigh unto the throne of God to govern all those planets which belong to the same order of that upon which you stand. And it is given unto you to know the set time of all the stars that are set to give light until you come near unto the throne of God.

3 Thus I, Abraham, talked with the Lord face to face, as one man talks with another, and he told me of the works which his hands had made. And he said unto me, My son, my son (and his hand was stretched out), behold, I will show you all these. And he put his hand upon my eyes, and I saw those things which his hands had made, which were many, and they multiplied before my eyes and I could not see the end thereof. And he said unto me, This is Shinehah, which is the sun. And he said unto me, Kokob, which is star. And he said unto me, Olea, which is the moon. And he said unto me, Kokaubeam, which signifies stars, or all the great lights which were in the firmament of heaven.

4 And it was in the night time when the Lord spoke these words unto me: I will multiply you, and your seed after you, like unto these; and if you can count the number of sands, so shall be the number of your seeds. And the Lord said unto me, Abraham, I show these things unto you, before you go into Egypt, that you may declare all these words. If two things exist, and there be one above the other, there shall be greater things above them. Therefore, Kolob is the greatest of all the kokaubeam that you have seen because it is nearest unto me. Now if there be two things, one above the other, and the moon be above the earth, then it may be that a planet or a star may exist above it. (And there is nothing that the Lord, your God, shall take in his heart to do but what he will do it.) Nevertheless, he made the greater star as, also, if there be two spirits and one shall be more intelligent than the other, yet these two spirits – notwithstanding one is more intelligent than the other – yet they have no beginning (they existed before), they shall have no end (they shall exist after), for they are gnolaum, or eternal. And the Lord said unto me, These two facts do exist – that there are two spirits, one being more intelligent than the other; there shall be another more

intelligent than they. I am the Lord, your God; I am more intelligent than they all. The Lord, your God, sent his angel to deliver you from the hands of the priest of Elkkener. I dwell in the midst of them all. I now therefore have come down unto you to deliver unto you the works which my hands have made, wherein my wisdom excels them all; for I rule in the heavens above and in the earth beneath, in all wisdom and prudence, over all the intelligences your eyes have seen from the beginning. I came down in the beginning in the midst of all the intelligences you have seen.

Chapter 6

Now the Lord had shown unto me, Abraham, the intelligences that were organized before the world was, and among all these there were many of the noble and great ones. And God saw these souls, that they were good, and he stood in the midst of them and he said, These I will make my rulers. For he stood among those that were spirits, and he saw that they were good. And he said unto me, Abraham, you are one of them; you were chosen before you were born.

2 And there stood one among them that was like unto God, and he said unto those who were with him, We will go down, for there is space there, and we will take of these materials and we will make an earth whereon these may dwell. And we will prove them herewith to see if they will do all things whatsoever the Lord their God shall command them. And they who keep their first estate shall be added upon, and they who keep not their first estate shall not have glory in the same kingdom with those who keep their first estate; and they who keep their second estate shall have glory added upon their heads for ever and ever.

3 And the Lord said, Who shall I send? And one answered like unto the Son of Man, Here am I, send me. And another answered and said, Here am I, send me. And the Lord said, I will send the first. And the second was angry and kept not his first estate, and at that day many followed after him.

Chapter 7

And then the Lord said, Let us go down. And they went down at the beginning and they organized and formed (that is, the Gods) the heavens and the earth. And the earth, after it was formed, was empty and desolate because they had not formed anything but the earth. And darkness reigned upon the face of the deep, and the spirit of the Gods was brooding upon the faces of the water.

2 And they said (the Gods), Let there be light. And there was light. And they (the Gods), comprehended the light, for it was bright. And they divided the light, or caused it to be divided, from the darkness, and the Gods called the light day, and the darkness they called night. And it came to pass that from the evening until morning they called night, and from the morning until the evening they called day. And this was the first, or the beginning, of that which they called day and night.

3 And the Gods also said, Let there be an expanse in the midst of the waters, and it shall divide the waters from the waters. And the Gods ordered the expanse so that it divided the waters which were under the expanse from the waters which were above the expanse. And it was so, even as they ordered. And the Gods called the expanse heaven. And it came to pass that it was from evening until morning that they called night. And it came to pass that it was morning until evening that they called day. And this was the second time that they called night and day.

4 And the Gods ordered, saying, Let the waters under the heaven be gathered together unto one place and let the earth come up dry. And it was so, as they ordered. And the Gods pronounced the earth dry, and the gathering together of the waters pronounced they great waters. And the Gods saw that they were obeyed. And the Gods said, Let us prepare the earth to bring forth grass, the herb yielding seed, the fruit tree yielding fruit after his kind, whose seed in itself yields its own likeness upon the earth. And it was so, even as they ordered. And the Gods organized the earth to bring forth grass from its own seed, and the herb to bring forth herb from its own seed, yielding seed after his kind, and the earth to bring forth the tree from its own seed, yielding fruit whose seed could only bring forth the same in itself, after his kind. And the Gods saw that they were obeyed. And it came to pass that they numbered the days: from the evening until the morning that they called night. And it came to pass from the morning until the evening they called day. And it was the third time.

5 And the Gods organized the lights in the expanse of the heaven, and caused them to divide the day from the night, and organized them to be for signs, and for seasons, and for days, and for years, and

organized them to be for lights in the expanse of the heaven to give light upon the earth. And it was so. And the Gods organized the two great lights, the greater light to rule the day and the lesser light to rule the night; with the lesser light, he set the stars also. And the Gods set them in the expanse of the heavens, to give light upon the earth, and to rule over the day and over the night, and to cause to divide the light from the darkness. And the Gods watched those things which they had ordered until they obeyed. And it came to pass that it was from evening until morning that it was night. And it came to pass that it was from morning until evening that it was day. And it was the fourth time.

6 And the Gods said, Let us prepare the waters to bring forth abundantly the moving creatures that have life, and the fowl that they may fly above the earth in the open expanse of heaven. And the Gods prepared the waters that they might bring forth great whales and every living creature that moves which the waters were to bring forth abundantly after their kind, and every winged fowl after their kind. And the Gods saw that they would be obeyed and that their plan was good. And the Gods said, We will bless them and cause them to be fruitful and multiply and fill the waters in the seas, or great waters, and cause the fowl to multiply in the earth. And it came to pass that it was from evening until morning that they called night. And it came to pass that it was from morning until evening that they called day. And it was the fifth time.

7 And the Gods prepared the earth to bring forth the living creature after his kind — cattle, and creeping things, and beasts of the earth after their kind. And it was so, as they had said. And the Gods organized the earth to bring forth the beasts after their kind, and cattle after their kind, and everything that creeps upon the earth after their kind. And the Gods saw they would obey. And the Gods took counsel among themselves, and said, Let us go down and form man in our image, after our likeness, and we will give them dominion over the fish of the sea, and over the fowl of the air, and over the cattle, and over all the earth, and over every creeping thing that creeps upon the earth. So the Gods went down to organize man in their own image, in the image of the Gods, to form they him — male and female, to form they them. And the Gods said, We will bless them. And the Gods said, We will cause them to be fruitful, and multiply, and replenish the earth, and subdue it, and to have dominion over the fish of the sea, and over the fowl of the air, and

over every living thing that moves upon the earth. And the Gods said, Behold, we will give them every herb bearing seed that shall come upon the face of all the earth and every tree which shall have fruit upon it – yea, the fruit of the tree yielding seed, to them we will give it; it shall be for their meat. And to every beast of the earth, and to every fowl of the air, and to everything that creeps upon the earth, behold, we will give them life, and also we will give to them every green herb for meat. And all these things shall be thus organized. And the Gods said, We will do everything that we have said and organize them, and behold, they shall be very obedient. And it came to pass that it was from evening until morning they called night. And it came to pass that it was from morning until evening they called day; and they numbered the sixth time.

8 And thus we will finish the heavens, and the earth, and all the hosts of them. And the Gods said among themselves, On the seventh time we will end our work which we have counseled, and we will rest on the seventh time from all our work which we have counseled. And the Gods concluded upon the seventh time, because that on the seventh time they would rest from all their works which they, the Gods, counseled among themselves to form, and sanctified it. And thus were their decisions at the time that they counseled among themselves to form the heavens and the earth. And the Gods came down and formed these, the generations of the heavens and of the earth, when they were formed in the day that the Gods formed the earth and the heavens, according to all that which they had said concerning every plant of the field before it was in the earth and every herb of the field before it grew. For the Gods had not caused it to rain upon the earth when they counseled to do them, and had not formed a man to till the ground. But there went up a mist from the earth and watered the whole face of the ground. And the Gods formed man from the dust of the ground, and took his spirit – that is, the man's spirit – and put it into him, and breathed into his nostrils the breath of life. And man became a living soul.

9 And the Gods planted a garden eastward in Eden, and there they put the man, whose spirit they had put into the body which they had formed. And out of the ground made the Gods to grow every tree that is pleasant to the sight and good for food; the Tree of Life also, in the midst of the garden, and the tree of knowledge of good and evil. There was a river running out of Eden to water the garden, and from thence it was parted and became into four heads.

10 And the Gods took the man and put him in the Garden of Eden to dress it and to keep it. And the Gods commanded the man, saying, Of every tree of the garden you may freely eat but of the tree of knowledge of good and evil. You shall not eat of it, for in the time that you eat thereof, you shall surely die. Now I, Abraham, saw that it was after the Lord's time, which was after the time of Kolob, for as yet the Gods had not appointed unto Adam his reckoning.

11 And the Gods said, Let us make a help meet for the man, for it is not good that the man should be alone. Therefore, we will form a help meet for him. And the Gods caused a deep sleep to fall upon Adam, and he slept. And they took one of his ribs and closed up the flesh in the stead thereof. And the rib, which the Gods had taken from man, formed they a woman and brought her unto the man. And Adam said, This was bone of my bones and flesh of my flesh; now she shall be called woman because she was taken out of man. Therefore shall a man leave his father and his mother and shall cleave unto his wife, and they shall be one flesh. And they were both naked, the man and his wife, and were not ashamed. And out of the ground the Gods formed every beast of the field, and every fowl of the air, and brought unto Adam to see what he would call them. And whatsoever Adam called every living creature, that should be the name thereof; and Adam gave names to all cattle, to the fowl of the air, to every beast of the field. And for Adam there was found a help meet for him.

Facsimile 2

A FACSIMILE FROM THE BOOK OF ABRAHAM
NO. 2

Explanation of the above cut

Fig. 1. Kolob, signifying the first creation, nearest to the celestial or the residence of God. First in government, the last pertaining to the measurement of time – the measurement according to the celestial time, which celestial time signifies one day to a cubit. One day in Kolob is equal to a thousand years according to the measurement of this earth, which is called by the Egyptians Jah-oh-eh.

Fig. 2. Stands next to Kolob, called by the Egyptians Oliblish, which is the next grand governing creation near to the celestial or the place where God resides; holding the key of power also pertaining to other planets, as revealed from God to Abraham as he offered sacrifice upon an altar which he had built unto the Lord.

Fig. 3. Is made to represent God sitting upon his throne, clothed with power and authority, with a crown of eternal light upon his head; representing also the grand keywords of the Holy Priesthood, as revealed to Adam in the Garden of Eden, as also to Seth, Noah, Melchizedek, Abraham and all to whom the Priesthood was revealed.

Fig. 4. Answers to the Hebrew word raukeeyang, signifying expanse, or the firmament of the heavens; also a numerical figure in Egyptian signifying one thousand, answering to the measuring of the time of Oliblish, which is equal with Kolob in its revolution and in its measuring of time.

Fig. 5. Is called in Egyptian Enish-go-on-dosh, that is, one of the governing planets also, and is said by the Egyptians to be the Sun and to borrow its light from Kolob through the medium of kae-e-vanrash, which is the grand key, or in other words, the governing power which governs fifteen other fixed planets or stars, as also floeese, or the moon, the earth, and the sun in their annual revolutions. This planet receives its power through the medium of Kli-flos-is-es, or Hah-ko-kau-beam, the stars represented by numbers 22 and 23 receiving light from the revolutions of Kolob.

Fig. 6. Represents this earth in its four quarters.

Fig. 7. Represents God sitting upon his throne, revealing, through the Heavens, the grand keywords of the Priesthood; as also, the sign of the holy ghost unto Abraham in the form of a dove.

Fig. 8. Contains writing that cannot be revealed unto the world, but is to be had in the holy temple of God.

Fig. 9. Ought not to be revealed at the present time.

Fig. 10. Also.

Fig. 11. Also. – If the world can find out these numbers, so let it be, Amen.

Figures 12, 13, 14, 15, 16, 17, 18, 19, and 21, will be given in the own due time of the Lord.

The above translation is given as far as we have any right to give at the present time

Facsimile 3

A FACSIMILE FROM THE BOOK OF ABRAHAM
NO. 3

Explanation of the above cut

Fig. 1. Abraham sitting upon Pharaoh's throne, by the politeness of the king, with a crown upon his head representing the Priesthood, as emblematical of the grand presidency in Heaven with the scepter of justice and judgment in his hand.

Fig. 2. King Pharaoh, whose name is given in the characters above his head.

Fig. 3. Signifies Abraham in Egypt, referring to Abraham as given in Figure 10 of Facsimile No. 1.

Fig. 4. Prince of Pharaoh, king of Egypt, as written above the hand.

Fig. 5. Shulem, one of the king's principal waiters, as represented by the characters above his hand.

Fig. 6. Olimlah, a slave belonging to the prince.

Abraham is reasoning upon the principles of astronomy in the king's court.

Additional Resources

The most accurate version of the Book of Abraham available is published as part of the new Restoration Edition of the Scriptures, Volume 3: Teachings & Commandments. It is available for free online at scriptures.info.

Denver Snuffer has authored numerous other books, including A Man Without Doubt (Amazon, 2016), which may be of interest to readers seeking to know more about Joseph Smith.

Readers can learn more about what God is doing to restore the gospel today by visiting TheTenTalks.com.

The Covenant mentioned in this book is available to review at ReceivetheCovenant.com.

www.ingramcontent.com/pod-product-compliance
Lightning Source LLC
Chambersburg PA
CBHW072028110526
44592CB00012B/1434